The Radical Challenge

**THE RESPONSE OF
SOCIAL DEMOCRACY**

The Radical Challenge

THE RESPONSE OF
SOCIAL DEMOCRACY

edited by
Alastair Kilmarnock

ANDRE DEUTSCH

First published 1987 by
André Deutsch Limited
105–106 Great Russell Street
London WC1

British Library Cataloguing in Publication Data

The Radical Challenge: the response of
social democracy.
1. Socialism — Great Britain
I. Kilmarnock, Alastair
320.5'315'0941   HX244

ISBN 0-233-98137-3

Printed in Great Britain by
Ebenezer Baylis & Son Ltd., Worcester

DEDICATION

In memory of Glenn S. Russell,
a prime mover and first secretary
of our political philosophy forum,
whose talents and enthusiasm were
sadly lost to us by his untimely
death at the age of twenty-six.

CONTENTS

INTRODUCTION

The Declaration for Social Democracy or Limehouse Declaration
issued on January 25th 1981 (most of which was later incorporated
in the preamble of the constitution of the Social Democratic Party)
set out 'to rally all those who are committed to the values, principles
and policies of social democracy'. After casting doubt on the
Labour Party's commitment to parliamentary democracy, it out-
lined its main objectives with a broad brush: it sought 'to reverse
Britain's economic decline'; it aimed at creating an 'open, classless
and more equal society'; it condemned 'the sterile and rigid framework' into which the British political system had fallen in the past
two decades; it rejected 'the politics of the inert centre'; it wanted
'more not less change in our society, but with a greater stability of
direction'; it advocated 'a healthy public sector and a healthy
private sector without frequent frontier changes'; it was determined
'to eliminate poverty and promote greater equality without stifling
enterprise or imposing bureaucracy from the centre'; it called for
'more decentralisation of decision making in industry and government, together with an effective system of democracy at work'; it did
not accept that mass unemployment was inevitable; it believed that
Britain should 'play a full and constructive role within the framework of the European Community, NATO, the United Nations and
the Commonwealth'.

Following the launch of the party in March of that year, these
aspirations attracted a very considerable number of people who had
previously belonged to no party and who joined, I think, not out of
attachment to any political theory but because the prospectus
'smelt' good – and that was enough for them to be going on with.
The party then matured and developed. It learned to campaign and
fight elections. It evolved a healthy democratic policy-making
mechanism, from which policies emerged in every conceivable area
of public action. Its support in the polls fluctuated. Whenever it
seemed to be doing well, it was accused by other parties of oppor-
tunism and lack of principle. This accusation immediately falls
down on a simple glance at the *Declaration for Social Democracy*
and it becomes especially absurd in the light of the appropriation of
some of the best ideas of the Social Democrats by those making the

accusation. However, it is the case that in a document of that length it was not possible to treat in any great depth the 'values and principles' invoked in it. It is also true that a political party is a complex body which operates on many levels; not only does it speak on the doorstep but, if its simpler messages are to carry conviction, it needs to be sure of its own roots and to be able to draw constant nourishment from them. Accordingly, it seemed to a number of us that it would be useful to set up a political philosophy forum, in which we could explore our political lineage, examine our links with Liberalism and develop the main propositions against which social democratic policies should be tested.

I became the convenor of our group and started the ball rolling by presenting my colleagues with a rather lengthy piece called 'The Empirical Tradition', which I do not reproduce here, as its main purpose was to stimulate other contributions. Suffice it to say that it set out by distinguishing broadly between the metaphysical and transcendental concepts native to the continent of Europe and the generally empirical thrust of British progressive political philosophy. It suggested that any new political initiative, such as the foundation and development of a new progressive party, would have to work within our native tradition deriving from Locke and the New Whigs and with the grain of British radical thinking rather than against it. At the same time, I found it hard to accept Benthamite utilitarianism, even with its subsequent refinements, as an adequate basis for the political critique mounted by the SDP. My paper attracted plenty of criticism, but whatever the shortcomings of my analysis it succeeded in one important respect: it stimulated the essays which appear in this book.

It may seem surprising that there are no contributions from prominent Liberals in the collection. The reasons are quite straightforward. The Liberal dimension is very fully taken into account and acknowledged in several of the essays, particularly those on utilitarianism, on the 'progressive tradition' and on Keynes. Liberal values are endorsed throughout the book, not least the moral imperative to assist those left behind by rapid and bewildering economic change. It must be recognised, however, that Social Democrats have converged from a different point of the compass, owing their origin to socialism, whose subsequent development in a statist and totalitarian direction led to the growth of revisionism and the triumph of modern German social democracy at Bad Godesberg in 1959. It was

Hugh Gaitskell's failure to perform the same operation on the British Labour Party – which remains committed to the common ownership of the means of production, distribution and exchange – that led ultimately to the formation of the SDP and ensures the new party of a continuing role for the foreseeable future. Labour's wooing of moderate opinion while Clause IV fundamentalism is still the official philosophy demonstrates a basic incoherence on which no sustained revival can be built. The need for a new post-socialist alternative to the Tories will become more not less pressing.

If there are enemies on the left, they are no less present on the right. I believe that one of the most important threads running through this collection is a refusal to accept the social and economic analysis of the 'New Right'. Owing to the vacuum in progressive thinking left by a conservative and inward-looking Labour Party, the New Right has undoubtedly dominated British political thinking for more than a decade. With gurus like Hayek, Friedman and Nozick, backed up by research institutes such as the Institute of Economic Affairs, the Adam Smith Institute and others, and aided by able *Spectator* journalists, it has seized and managed to hold the commanding heights of the political argument. It has successfully given birth to a political movement, Thatcherism, which aspires to continue in power well into the next decade, if not into the next century. This movement has also been called the Radical Right. Invoking free markets and private enterprise as its principles, it set out to curb trade union power, municipal imperialism and corporatist collusion, which it saw as sapping the British economy and weakening the springs of competition. Few would deny that there were abuses crying for reform. Thus there was a *Radical Challenge*. But this has been taken up by the Tories in a highly partisan and sectarian, not to say punitive spirit, leading to blatant increases in inequalities of income and wealth and vastly widening the economic differences between regions in a relatively small island. These distorted results of Tory reforms have not responded humanely or even efficiently to the original challenge, which therefore remains, reformulated perhaps, but more than ever demanding an answer if Britain is to shake off the blight that threatens to condemn her to an endless prospect of social disorder and relative economic decline.

In offering an alternative response and gaining acceptance for an alternative strategy, the new Social Democratic Party, in alliance with the Liberals, has encountered some of the classic difficulties confronting parties of the centre, none of which is glossed over in this book. Not least among the hurdles for the new party has been the unfamiliar ring of its name in the average British voter's ear. As a phrase, 'social democracy' has long been a commonplace among cognoscenti to describe a broad swathe of political opinion shared by a number of continental parties and equally covering the approach of both main British parties during the consensus years. But something sharper has obviously been required and expected since the phrase suddenly turned up, as from 1981, in the name of a party and as part of the current vocabulary and day-to-day coinage of British politics. Therefore, the book opens with Roger Morgan's essay, in which he sets the SDP in perspective, traces the continental branch of its ancestry and shows where both the new party and the old Labour Party stand on six main policy issues in relation to the mainstream of the European non-communist left.

On the domestic front David Marquand then examines the specifically British 'progressive tradition' and asks why all the 'middle way' programmes have ultimately failed, while in other democracies they have met with considerable success. I will not spoil his pitch by revealing the answer. The four following essays by George Goyder, Alan Ryan, Mark Goyder and Robert Skidelsky look respectively at Adam Smith, J.S. Mill, John Ruskin and J.M. Keynes, exploring their relationships with and effect on progressive thought. Robert Skidelsky addresses the question whether we should any longer be constrained by Keynes's 'institutional timidity' in our approach to institutional reform. Next, Inigo Bing and Kevin Carey focus our attention on American liberalism, especially as manifested in the work of John Rawls. They are followed by Dorothy Emmet, who warns against the adoption of any single exclusive philosophical system and graphically demonstrates the interaction between the 'moral' and the 'power and interests' views of democracy. The last two essays are more overtly 'political'. Danny Finkelstein explores Labour revisionism and clarifies the crucial distinction between so-called 'democratic socialism' and British democracy. Finally, Nick Bosanquet launches a counterattack on the New Right, recapturing many of the heights of the political debate (only occupied by the Right through the lack of any coherent challenge from the traditional Left) and staking out quite clearly the social democratic position.

In presenting these essays I have striven to reflect as far as possible the procedure we followed ourselves. Our method was simple and direct. We met (and still meet) approximately once a month, when a paper that has been previously circulated is introduced by its author and then discussed. Rather than planning this series, we found it grew organically, each discussion revealing the need for a further paper to carry forward our work of appraisal and development of our position. A condensed record of each discussion is taken; these are not reproduced here because they would double the length of the book. But I have drawn on them for the linking passages that are intended to build a bridge for the reader from one piece to the next.

I should make it clear at the outset that the contributions to this collection do not all approach Britain's ills from an identical viewpoint. The book is essentially about the revival of liberal democracy but does not disguise the difficulties; rather than sailing on a constant course with a following wind it tacks towards its goal. Some authors set off empirically from a basically utilitarian standpoint, albeit with modifications; others argue for a more contractual or 'rights-based' framework for our social and economic relationships. I shall not, in summing up at the end, attempt to impose any artificial uniformity on these views. Their strength lies in their convergence on similar conclusions. Sensible empiricists wanting a stable and prosperous society will accede to claims that others prefer to call rights. Nonetheless, it is wrong to sit on the fence in the arguments between 'rights' on the one hand and 'goals' on the other. So, at the very end, I shall suggest just how far down the 'rights' road a progressive political movement with a strong practical streak should venture. It is the hope and belief of all who have collaborated in this volume that the reader will emerge at the end with an enhanced sense of the values common to British social democrats.

ONE

Continental Social Democracy
Political Philosophy and Political Practice

ROGER MORGAN

In taking the name Social Democratic Party, the British SDP has indicated its affiliation to a well-established continental tradition of political philosophy and political action. A well-established tradition, but also an ambiguous one: what has 'social democracy' meant in continental thinking, and what does it mean today?

Philosophically all social democrats certainly start with Marx and his antecedents. In *German Social Democracy* (1896) Bertrand Russell quotes Engels as follows: 'We German Socialists are proud of our descent, not only from Saint-Simon, Fourier and Owen, but also from Kant, Fichte and Hegel. The German Labour Movement is the heir of German Classic Philosophy.' Russell comments: 'This haughty claim gives to Social Democracy an interest and a human value beyond that of any ordinary political movement. For Social Democracy is not a mere political party, nor even a mere economic theory; it is a complete self-contained philosophy of the world and of human development'.[1]

The inevitability of the collapse of capitalism was the main determinist thrust behind the Marxist philosophy of the early social democrats. Revisionist arguments by Edward Bernstein and others, dating from the 1890s, when Russell was writing his book, include more references to Kant. Thus, social democracy has remained, as it began, a slightly ambiguous phrase.

The expression 'Social Democracy in Europe' formed the title of a pamphlet by the late Anthony Crosland – a lecture organised by the Socialist International in Costa Rica in October 1975 and later published by the Fabian Society[2] – and Crosland's text illustrates most usefully the extreme ambiguity of the concept of social democracy. Even though one of his close associates has recently stated that Crosland, 'one of the most articulate and persuasive social-democratic theorists of his generation, used indignantly to repudiate the description as historically inaccurate and philosophically vacuous',[3] Crosland himself did not hestiate, in his 1975 lecture, to describe himself and his Labour colleagues of the time as 'members of a social democratic government in Europe', and in the course of his lecture he used 'social democracy', 'revisionist social democracy' and 'socialism' as interchangeable terms. In a brief but incisive discussion of the European member-parties of the International, Crosland referred comprehensively to the Social Democratic Parties of Sweden, West Germany and Austria, the French Socialist Party, and his own Labour Party as representatives of 'European Social Democracy'[4].

In view of the way history has treated some of these parties since Crosland wrote – the French Socialist Party finding itself for a time in coalition with a Communist Party which has always denounced social democrats as renegades, and Crosland's own party under-going a breakaway of moderates who reproach it with being not nearly social democratic enough – a clarification of this terminology and its implications is overdue.

Historically, the relationship between the concepts 'social' and 'democratic' can be traced back to the European revolutionary movements of 1848. One of these transnational movements – indeed the main one, along with the force of nationalism – was the demand for democratic government, against the prevailing power of auto-cracy. In a period of history when the main aim of progressive movements was the achievement of democracy, the workers and idealists who strove for socialism, or even for the recognition of 'the social question' were in a small minority. The term 'social democrat' thus came to be applied to this minority of democrats who also stood for socialism: one of the earliest publications to be called *The Social Democrat* was the journal of the first German socialist party, the General German Workers' Association founded by Ferdinand Lassalle in 1863. One of the ironies of the nomenclature of working-class parties is that Marx himself, observing and trying to influence the German scene from his London exile, was pleased when his own followers baptised their own party – founded at the Eisenach Congress in 1869 – the Social Democratic Workers' Party; he indig-nantly rebuked them for agreeing in 1875 (when the Gotha Congress united them with the Lassalleans) to accept the title of Socialist Workers' Party, which he regarded as tactically and historically inappropriate.[5]

It was at the Halle and Erfurt Congresses of 1890-1 that the German party adopted its present title of Social Democratic Party of Germany (*Sozialdemokratische Partei Deutschlands*), and a programme drafted largely by Karl Kautsky, of which many traces were to remain until the historic Godesberg Congress of 1959. In the 1890s the SPD established itself as the dominant party in the Second International (founded in Paris in 1889),[6] and the name Social Democratic Party was at about this time adopted, sometimes in imitation, by parties in smaller countries including Austria, the Scandinavian countries and Holland (also of course in Tsarist Russia, where Bolsheviks and Mensheviks were wings of a social democratic party). H.M. Hyndman's Social Democratic Federation became the first party to bear the label in Britain, but it adopted a dogmatic version of Marxism which placed it out of line both with the pragmatic development of socialism in Britain (then mainly Fabian, of course) and with the more flexible interpretations of Marxist doctrine by Kautsky and Bernstein.

A further complication of terminology occurred when 'social democracy' came to be applied to the organised political movement itself, as well as to its goal. When the young Bertrand Russell published his first book, *German Social Democracy*, in 1896 (basing it on material collected by frequenting SPD meetings while staying with his kinsman the British Ambassador in Berlin, and presented first as a series of lectures at the newly-founded London School of Economics) what he meant by social democracy was, as in the then current German usage, the party and its supporters.[7] The same was of course true of Edward Bernstein's historic work *The Preconditions of Socialism and the Tasks of Social Democracy* (*Die Voraussetzungen des Sozialismus und die Aufgaben der Sozialdemokratie*), published in 1899: he was discussing the tasks facing the SPD. And Lenin himself wrote *What is to be done?*, the manifesto for a new kind of party, as a member of the Russian Social Democratic Party.

The doctrine of social democracy was by now developing into a variety of schools: in Germany Kautsky represented a revolutionary orthodoxy (through it was heavily marked by tactical considerations) against Bernstein's quasi-Fabian insistence that gradualism was not only right but inevitable, whereas in Vienna the 'Austro-Marxist' school was beginning to develop an approach that was at the same time more revolutionary and more humane and imaginative. The fundamental turning-point, however, came with the

Bolshevik Revolution and its sequel in the establishment of the Communist (or Third) International. By imposing the famous twenty-one conditions for acceptance into the Comintern in 1920, Lenin and his colleagues marked a final division between the communist parties and the socialist or social-democratic forces of the old Second International which were not prepared to accept the Bolshevik principles of party organisation and policy. It was at this point that 'social democratic' took on its current international meaning: instead of social democrats being the democrats who were also socialists, as in 1848, they were henceforth the socialists who were also committed to democracy in the liberal parliamentary sense.

For the last sixty years the label 'social democratic' has been applied to the family of European parties between the Communists to the Left and the Liberals or Christian Democrats to the Right. The term has been used, as by Crosland, to cover parties as diverse as those in Germany, Austria, Scandinavia, France and Britain, and it is important to look in more detail at the objectives which these very diverse parties have actually pursued.

One of the central factors influencing this (and further confirming the widening split between communism and social democracy in the inter-war years and again since 1945) has been that in many countries of Europe social democratic parties have held governmental power, usually but not always in coalition with others. (Before 1914 socialists were always parties of opposition. Edward Grey's lament when war came – 'This is the end of everything. We shall have Labour governments everywhere after this!' – was perceptive, if exaggerated.) Thus the SPD took on ministerial office in Berlin during the opening and closing years of the Weimar Republic (between 1919 and 1923, and again between 1928 and 1930); in Vienna, social democrats held office during most of the troubled history of the First Austrian Republic (1918 to 1934); in Sweden, the social democrats' victory in 1932 was to put them into office for more than forty years; and even in France and Spain, where the Left was fatally divided between socialists and communists, the 1930s saw brief periods of Popular Front government under socialist leadership.

By 1945, when the postwar years brought a renewed period of social democratic government in large parts of Western Europe, one of the fundamental differences separating social democracy from communism (or indeed from left-wing socialism) had become absolutely clear: communists and many others continued to define 'socialism' in the traditional terms of ownership of the means of production. Parties like the German, Austrian or Scandinavian social democrats, who had decisively abandoned this view to embrace the idea of a mixed economy, including both public and private sectors, were denounced by the Left (including the communists and significant elements in the socialist parties in France, Italy, Britain and Greece) for 'managing the capitalist system' rather than making the transition to 'socialism'. The leaders of the successful social democratic parties were able to argue in reply that the economic systems over which they presided at least provided impressively for the needs of most of their citizens (and that the question whether they were labelled 'mixed economy' or 'welfare capitalism' was irrelevant), and also that the social democratic formula continued to hold the confidence of democratic electorates. This, of course, has always been a fundamental principle for a movement which regards representative democracy as one of its essential values.[8]

Indeed, until the economic storms of the 1970s, which have placed all European political systems under new pressures and revived the traditional debate about the viability of capitalism, the social democrats could fairly claim to be the natural party of government over wide stretches of Western Europe. In Sweden, their forty uninterrupted years of office only ended in the mid-1970s. In Austria, they have enjoyed the permanent status of a government party ever since 1945. In West Germany, after several years during which their power was confined to the city and regional levels, they were permanently in national office under Brandt and Schmidt from 1966 to 1982. And in smaller countries, in Scandinavia, the Low Countries, and Switzerland, parties of the social democratic persuasion have very often played an important part in government coalitions. Right up to the early 1980s it could be argued that the successful socialist parties of Europe were the social democratic ones, and that the parties still tied to nineteenth-century ideas about socialism and capitalism had less to show for their efforts. Even though there were obvious reasons for the desperate weakness of the socialist parties in the three Mediterranean dictatorships, Spain, Greece and Portugal, the situation in more favoured parts of Europe was hardly brighter.

In France, the Socialist Party, despite the doctrinal purity imposed in 1947 by its General Secretary Guy Mollet, had participated mainly in Centre-Right coalitions under the Fourth Republic, before its banishment to apparently permanent opposition in the 1960s and 1970s, including briefly the fragile pact with the communists in 1972, calamitously broken off by the latter in 1977. In Italy, where democratic socialism was handicapped not only by the crushing predominance of the Communist Party but also by the endemic split between its own social democratic and socialist wings, there had been occasional minor contributions to coalition governments but little more. And in Britain, as the achievements of the 1945–51 Labour government faded into the past and the conflict over Clause IV of the constitution ended in a deadlock (Gaitskell failed to end the party's commitment to nationalisation, and Wilson and Callaghan failed to put it into practice), it was hard to argue that the intermittent Labour governments of the 1960s and 1970s had come effectively to grips with Britain's problems.

This picture of the strengths and weaknesses of European socialism – 'social democratic' parties doing fairly well in the German-speaking areas and Scandinavia, and more strictly 'socialist' parties condemned to frustrating impotence in France, the Mediterranean countries and (perhaps) Britain – has been modified by the developments of the 1980s. On the one hand, the fortunes of German and Scandinavian social democracy suffered in the economic troubles of this period, which brought swings to the Right in Stockholm (briefly), Oslo, West Berlin and Bonn. On the other hand, the more explicitly socialist parties of France, Greece and Spain saw a revival of their electoral fortunes, and took office with high hopes of promoting fundamental economic and social change. However, the constraints they faced, once in power, obliged them to limit their ambitions and to pursue policies of an essentially social democratic nature.

Indeed, the international economic recession which has dominated European politics since the mid-1970s has done more than any other single factor to challenge the assumptions of all left-wing parties, and to test the capacity of 'social democratic' and 'socialist' governments alike to find a solution. As the automatic assumption of continued growth and full employment was swept away by the facts of recession, both the social democratic approach to national economic management (as in West Germany, Austria and Scandinavia) and the socialist approach of greater state control (as in France and Greece) have proved to be only partially successful.[9]

The effect of the recession on the party programmes of the Left and Centre-Left has been to stimulate revised versions of the established policy preferences, in which, however, the traditional distinction between 'socialist' and 'social democratic' approaches is clearly visible. The issue of public ownership versus the mixed economy has been repeatedly used here and elsewhere as the most obvious yardstick for distinguishing 'socialists' from 'social democrats' in today's Europe. It is necessary to place this issue in the context of others which are important, and on which socialists and social democrats offer a range of different answers. How do the parties of Europe's non-communist Left stand on the main policy issues of the 1980s? And how do the British Labour Party and its new rival the SDP fit into the spectrum of European socialism and social democracy as a whole?

In the table which follows, the attitudes of a number of European parties towards six central issues of policy are tabulated. The parties selected are the social democratic parties now in opposition in Paris and Bonn; the British Labour Party and SDP; the social democratic parties of two neutral states, Austria and Sweden; and the PASOK, now in power in Greece. (For comparison, the French and Italian Communist Parties are also included.)

The policy issues chosen as most important comprise three of an essentially domestic character (nationalisation, economic planning, and welfare spending), and three external ones (the European Community, defence and relations with the 'third world'). These isues have been selected not only for their importance, but because they usefully illustrate the critical differences between the parties concerned. Even when their attitudes, summarily expressed, appear similar (as for instance their unanimous 'yes' to concern for the third world), the actual substance of their respective policies varies considerably. Some other issues which are of great importance in one or more of the countries (e.g. electoral reform, private schooling, or relations with the Communist Party) have been omitted because they are irrelevant elsewhere; issues such as industrial democracy or the party constitution, which arise in very different forms in different countries, have not been included either.

In considering the table it must be recalled that it presents a very summary view of a highly complex subject, in the sense that the precise policy of a party is often difficult to pin down with a yes or a no: these monosyllabic entries give only an approximate summary

POSITIONS OF EUROPEAN PARTIES ON MAJOR ISSUES

	1 Extension of public ownership	2 More economic planning	3 Increased welfare spending	4 Commitment to European Community	5 Nuclear defence and multilateral disarmament	6 Concern for third world
PS	Yes	Yes	Yes	Yes	Yes (not NATO)	Yes
SPD	No	Not much	No?	Yes	Yes (no national nuclear arms)	Yes
Labour Party	Yes	Yes	Yes	No	No	Yes
SDP	No	Not much	No?	Yes	Yes	Yes
OSP (Austria)	No	Yes?	No?	N/A	N/A	Yes
SAP (Sweden)	No	Yes?	No?	N/A	Not NATO or nuclear: multilateral, yes	Yes
PASOK	Yes	Yes	Yes	No?	No?	Yes
PCI	Yes	Yes	Yes	Yes	Yes?	Yes
PCF	Yes	Yes	Yes	No	No?	Yes

of complex realities. For instance, the 'concern for the third world' to which all the parties are reported as saying 'yes' means something different as between France and Germany, or between Sweden and Greece. Again, the positive commitment to the European Community, as spelled out in recent statements by say François Mitterrand, Helmut Schmidt and Roy Jenkins, inevitably covers a wide spectrum of ideas about Europe; the reticence about 'increased welfare spending' of several parties may be a reaction to current financial stringency rather than a matter of fundamental principle; 'more economic planning' for some parties might be acceptable if it meant the securing of national energy supplies, but not the *dirigiste* location of industry; and so forth. However, in general terms the table gives an indication of the way the parties tend to point.

The most important aspects of these entries, as far as both the position of the British parties and the future of the European Community are concerned, are the comparisons to be made among the positions of the parties in Britain, France and Germany, the three leading countries of the Community. (The comparisons with the parties in Austria, Sweden, and Greece are also instructive, but less crucial.) Considering first the three areas of domestic policy (columns 1, 2 and 3), the main division is clearly between the French Socialist Party and the British Labour Party on the one hand – both of them committed to the extension of nationalisation, to economic planning, and to increased public spending – and on the other hand the Social Democratic Parties in Germany and Britain, which share the opposing view on all three points. It is true that there are differences as well as similarities between the French Socialist Party and the British Labour Party in regard to nationalisation for instance: in France the continuing commitment to nationalisation is motivated partly by the tactical need for the PS to outmanoeuvre the Communist Party, and partly by the self-confidence of a tradition of successful state-run enterprises that reaches back beyond the success story of Renault to the enterprises of Sully and Colbert, whereas on this point the Labour Party is more defensive. However, the approaches to economic policy of the two parties have much in common, including the protectionist elements in the Labour Party's 'alternative economic strategy' and the declaration by President Mitterrand in 1981 that nationalisation in France was designed partly to insulate the country from the ill-effects of 'the international division of labour'. Again, a comparison between the apparent positions of the

SPD and the SDP on economic issues shows differences as well as similarities: however, it is fair to say that on this point the overall approach of the two parties is very similar.

If we turn to the issues of external policy in columns 4, 5 and 6 (though it is highly questionable to apply this term to the issue of the European Community), the dividing lines between the four parties run in a different pattern. They are all committed to the principle of good relations with the third world (column 6), though further inspection would reveal big differences on what this concept actually means. On the Community and defence, however, the dividing-line runs in a way which places the British Labour Party on one side, and all the other three on the other. There are differences between them, to be sure. On defence, there are important distinctions to be made between the French Socialist Party (strongly committed to the *force de frappe* and to the Western alliance, though not to NATO as such), the SPD (non-nuclear but devoutly committed to NATO, including its current policy on nuclear forces in the European theatre), and the SDP (pro-NATO, pro-Polaris but anti-Trident, and strongly pro-multilateral disarmament): but all three approaches stand in contrast to the unilateralism of the Labour Party. On the issue of the European Community it needs no underlining that the French view, which envisages an interventionist and *dirigiste* Community actively promoting industrial and regional policies (a view which Messrs Mauroy, Cheysson and Chandernagor have inherited from an earlier generation of the French Left, represented by Uri, Hirsch, and Marjolin), is in clear contrast to the more free-enterprise-orientated approach of Messrs Schmidt, Matthöfer or Corterier (on this issue, the British SDP has on the whole situated itself somewhere between the French and German positions). However, the important point is again that the PS, SPD and SDP are all committed to making the Community work and to tackling their countries' problems within it, whereas the Labour Party is committed in principle to taking Britain out of it.

Events move fast, and it should be repeated that the actual policies the parties will pursue in future cannot be precisely predicted, but there is enough evidence to give a provisional answer to the question posed above, namely how the Labour Party and the SDP stand in relation to the mainstream of the European non-communist Left. On economic issues, the Labour Party is on almost every point aligned with the French Socialist Party against the consensus which includes the SPD, the SDP and the social democrats of Austria and Scandinavia (indeed, the Labour Party is in line with the Socialist Party of Greece on both economic and foreign policy issues, and also with the French Communist Party). On the questions of defence and the European Community, the Labour Party is at odds with the German and the French parties: the SDP is firmly within their framework of thinking.

The Social Democratic Party, in fact, seems to be developing in a way which is true to its title: the title is a familiar one in the history of other European countries, though not of Britain, and the challenge which the SDP has set itself can be seen not only as the breaking of the current British political mould, but also as its replacement by something more akin to the patterns of the continent.

DISCUSSION ON ONE

Speaking to his paper, Roger Morgan said that as a result of recent setbacks to social democracy Marxism was mounting a new critique, which had forced social democrats to rethink their position. The idea of a 'social market economy' (a phrase coined by the Christian Democrats under Erhard) had been refloated by David Owen as the 'social market', which appeared to indicate the application of market disciplines to the delivery of social services. But the German interpretation had been that of a market economy with a concern for social problems, in which economic growth was to be relied on to fund the provision of these collective services.

In discussion it was suggested that Britain had never been very interested in growth; no single British political philosopher had ever come fully to terms with the Industrial Revolution; industry remained a second-rate affair, employing second-class citizens; we had never been wholly at ease with our industrial past. When it was objected that it was pushing things a bit far to say that the British economic tradition had no concern for economics, this was countered by the contention that there had never been any deep analysis; Tawney, Hobson and co were peddling nostalgia, not economic thinking; hence Labour's schizophrenia over Clause IV, which had never been resolved, leaving them in the totally irreconcilable position of commitment both to total public ownership and to a mixed economy; it was one of the roles of the SDP to develop a coherent attitude towards profit.

Of the presence of Marx and Kant in the historical genealogy of social democracy there could be no reasonable doubt; the great lesson of Marx was that you could not ignore the economic substructure of social relationships; Marx's analysis of the brutality of the early Industrial Revolution was correct; he was undoubtedly the great 'structural sociologist'; Evan Durbin and Tony Crosland would certainly not have written as they did without their Marxist roots. The suggestion was made that, if you looked closely at the liberal tradition, you began to see how much the SDP owed to European social democracy and to socialism; social democracy everywhere had more confidence than liberalism in the power of the state. Against this the point was made that there was a strong strand of liberal statism too: there was plenty of intervention in the *Yellow Book* of 1928*. From another quarter it was argued that, even if the debt to socialism was acknowledged, the SDP was to be distinguished from the main socialist tradition based on economic analysis because it was closer to the British progressive tradition – which was more concerned with democracy itself as a basis of values.

Roger Morgan had ended his talk on the note that the SDP should be seeking to replace the current British political mould with something more akin to the patterns of the continent. At the same time, considerable differences between the British and continental traditions had emerged in discussion. It was therefore decided that a paper was required to define the British progressive tradition and appraise its strengths and weaknesses: David Marquand agreed to undertake this task.

*The *Yellow Book* is the popular term for the Liberal Party's publication, *Britain's Industrial Future*, London, 1928.

TWO

Phoenix from the Ashes
Revising the Progressive Tradition

DAVID MARQUAND

For about thirty years from the end of the Second World War, Britain's political and economic leaders shared a broadly similar approach to the management of the economy, to the relationship between the public and private sectors and to the principles governing welfare policy. To be sure, the two great parties differed vigorously about the details of policy; on a deeper level, they also differed about the nature of the good society and the springs of political authority. But they argued out their differences within a remarkably stable framework of common assumptions and common priorities. Both party leaderships accepted the full-employment commitment of the wartime coalition's famous 1944 white paper on employment policy. Both took it for granted that the Keynesian revolution in economic thought provided the techniques through which policy makers could honour that commitment in practice. Both wished to maintain a mixed economy, in which a substantial public sector co-existed with a still predominant private sector. Both were committed to the welfare state, substantially – if not in every detail – on the lines laid down in the 1942 Beveridge report and enacted by the post-war Labour government.

By the standards of the past, that consensus was astonishingly successful. For most of the post-war period, the economy grew faster than ever before. More important still, Britain became a fairer, kinder and less class-conscious society, as well as a richer one. Yet the consensus has plainly broken down. Plainly, too, its breakdown has put heavy strain on some of the most cherished features of the 'Westminster model' of parliamentary government, and called into question many of the assumptions which have given that model its persuasive power and legitimating force. The reasons for the breakdown, however, are not plain at all. On one level, no doubt, the explanation is straightforward. Despite rapid growth by previous British standards, the economy grew much more slowly than those of most developed countries; because of this, Britain turned out to be much more vulnerable to the shocks of the 1970s than were most of her competitors. The sight of successive consensus governments grappling unsuccessfully with repeated balance-of-payments crises, unprecedented currency depreciation, endemic inflation and mounting unemployment could hardly fail to give new plausibility to the criticisms of the neo-liberals on their right and the neo-socialists on their left. But to say that economic failure was responsible for the collapse of the consensus only pushes the question one stage further back. What we need to know in that case is why the economy failed.

Despite their obvious differences, the neo-socialists and neo-liberals offer an uncannily similar analysis. For both, capitalism is capitalism and socialism, socialism. For both, the whole notion of a mixed system, combining elements of traditional capitalism and traditional socialism in a synthesis more benign than either, is, and always has been, an absurdity. Both hold that the consensus collapsed because the policies it engendered were doomed to fail – either because they could not resolve the inherent contradictions of capitalism, or because they were bound, in the long run, to generate excessive demands on the part of the populace and excessive commitments on the part of the state.[1] Though these explanations contain obvious elements of truth, they go too wide. Policies not unlike those pursued by Britain's consensus politicians were pursued at the same time in most of north-western Europe and North America. If the British policies were doomed to failure, so were their foreign equivalents. But the ideological polarisation which destroyed the post-war consensus in this country has had no real parallel in the rest of north-western Europe;[2] and nor have the economic failures which precipitated it. Though Thatcherism has a transatlantic equivalent, it and Bennism are both home-grown. Their roots are to be found at home as well; and so are the roots of the crises to which they were a response.

II

The rise, decline and possible revival of what I have decided to call the 'progressive tradition' in British politics – in other words, the current of thought and feeling from which the politicians and intellectuals of the post-war consensus drew their inspiration – should be examined against this background. The progressive tradition was, of course, inexplicit and heterogeneous. It can be traced back, from the post-war Labour 'revisionists' and their Conservative equivalents, to the 'New Liberals' who provided the justification and rationale for the social reforms of the 1906 Liberal government; to 'One Nation' Conservatives, like Harold Macmillan and R.A. Butler, who traced their own intellectual ancestry back to Benjamin Disraeli and the 'Young England' Tories of the 1840s; and to the 'New Fabians' of the inter-war period, who tried to revise and toughen the messy amalgam of populist radicalism, trade-unionist sectionalism and gradualist socialism which had come so ignominiously to grief under the second Labour government. As all this implies, it has never been confined to a single party; perhaps because of this, its adherents were often more conscious of the party ambitions and loyalties which divided them than of the deeper, often only half-conscious assumptions and values which they had in common. No doubt for the same reason, historians and political scientists have paid surprisingly little attention to it.[3] Labour historians have been anxious to assess the place of its Labour adherents in a Labour or socialist tradition; historians of the Conservative Party have examined the influence on its Conservative adherents of previous Conservative politicians and thinkers. In doing so, they have focused attention on the divisions within it. This essay starts from the assumption that, if we are to understand the part which its adherents have played in recent British history – and, in particular, their inability to overcome the long drawn out economic decline which culminated first in the economic failures of the 1970s and then in the eclipse of the tradition itself – it is more fruitful to focus on what they had in common.

Five common features stand out. In the first place, New Liberals, One Nation Conservatives and New Fabians were all children of the technological and economic transformation of the late-nineteenth and early-twentieth centuries, which had undermined the foundations of Britain's informal, free-trade empire and invalidated many of the assumptions of the classical market liberalism of the Industrial Revolution.[4] Secondly, each of these three strands of opinion was consciously trying to revise its own particular tradition in the light of this transformation. Thirdly, each reached the conclusion – though not always in these words – that, in the new economic environment with which it was trying to come to terms, the 'invisible hand' of the classical political economists no longer worked as it was supposed to work, and that, because of this, it was no longer true that resources should be allocated by market forces alone. Fourthly, each also came to accept an under-consumptionist macro-economic analysis, according to which depression and unemployment were the products, at least in part, of deficient demand, which could be put right by pump priming on the part of the state, rather than, as classical market liberalism implied, of imperfections in the labour market, which could be put right only by stripping organised labour of its power to cause them. Finally, each saw the kind of managed welfare capitalism and mixed economy which actually came into being under the post-war Labour government, not as a *pis aller* imposed by adverse circumstances, but as positively desirable on its own account.

Five texts convey the flavour. The first is L.T. Hobhouse's master-piece of lucid compression, *Liberalism*, first published in 1911. This serves two purposes. It is a dispassionate account of the development of liberal thought and practice. It is also a subtle, though not wholly successful, attempt to justify the new, 'social' liberalism of the 1906 Liberal government in terms of the historic liberalism of the nineteenth century – to conduct, as it were, a kind of ideological marriage service between David Lloyd George and John Stuart Mill. Liberalism, Hobhouse asserts, is about liberty. Hence, the historic Liberal commitment to civil, religious and political liberty and, in the economic sphere, to free trade. But liberty is not a good in itself. Liberals value it, not for its own sake, but because they recognise that it is a prerequisite of the personal growth which is, in turn, a prerequisite of social harmony: because Liberalism

> is the belief that society can safely be founded on the self-directing power of personality, that it is only on this foundation that a true community can be built . . . Liberty then becomes not so much a right of the individual as a necessity of society. It rests not on the claim of A to be let alone by B, but on the duty of B to treat A as a rational being.[5]

The 'self-directing power of personality' cannot flower, however, unless the 'normal healthy citizen' can maintain himself; and, as things are, this is, and will remain, impossible. Despite a marked improvement in social conditions since the 1840s, the average working man does not enjoy the degree of economic independence necessary for the realisation of the liberal ideal; and there is little prospect that he will ever be able to enjoy it in the kind of economy which currently exists. On the contrary, 'the system of industrial competition . . . holds out no hope of an improvement which shall bring the means of such a healthy and independent existence as should be the birthright of every citizen of a free state within the grasp of the mass of the people of the United Kingdom.'[6] State intervention is therefore necessary to provide access to the means of production, for example by land settlement, and to guarantee the individual 'a certain share in the common stock' through the taxation of socially-created wealth. Such intervention is not an infringement of individual liberty, for socially-created wealth rightly belongs to society, not to the individuals who happen currently to possess it.

For Hobhouse, then, social liberalism was above all a matter of redistribution. Market forces alone would not provide the average wage earner with a decent standard of living; the state should therefore step in to modify market outcomes. But there was no suggestion in his writings – or, for that matter, in the policies actually followed by the Liberal government of the day – that market forces could not produce sufficient wealth *in toto*. In his system, state intervention was needed only to ensure equitable consumption; he did not challenge the classical assumption that the undistorted competitive market would maximise production. After the First World War, however, a new note appears in social liberal thinking – most notably (and most impressively) in the famous *Yellow Book* of 1928, which provided the intellectual foundations for Lloyd George's election campaign a year later. Where the pre-war social liberals had focused on consumption, the *Yellow Book* focused on production: on the inefficiencies of the market, rather than on its inequities.

In the first place, it set out a proto-Keynesian programme of pump priming to stimulate employment, through infrastructure spending on roads, waterways and land reclamation. More importantly, it also proposed an elaborate scheme of micro-economic intervention to improve the supply side of the economy, including profit sharing, wider share ownership and the establishment of works councils in all concerns with more than fifty employees; a National Investment Board; an Economic General Staff; and a Council of Industry with representatives from government, employers and unions to 'keep under continuous review the movement of wage rates and direct the attention of negotiating bodies to undesirable disparities'. Buttressing all this was a set of arguments to justify such intervention, two of which deserve particular attention. The first was that Britain's economic problems were rooted in 'outworn methods, ideas [and] traditions' – in other words, that market actors do not always know their own business best, and that state intervention may be necessary to correct their mistakes. The second was that 'the supposed choice between Individualism and Socialism is largely an obsolete issue'; and that although the market was unrivalled as a test of comparative efficiency, public (though not necessarily state) ownership should be introduced in spheres where private enterprise could not raise capital for undertakings of national importance, or where the private shareholder no longer performed a useful function.[7]

Younger members of the two big parties were moving in the same direction. As far back as 1927, four Conservative MPs, Oliver Stanley, Robert Boothby, Harold Macmillan and John de V. Loder, published a kind of interventionist manifesto, entitled *Industry and the State*, calling for more government action to promote industrial amalgamation and improve industrial relations, in particular through co-partnership between employers and workers.[8] The most important expression of this vein in inter-war Conservative thought came a decade later, with Harold Macmillan's *The Middle Way*, published in 1938. Like the authors of the Liberal *Yellow Book*, Macmillan advocated Keynesian pump priming to increase demand and reduce unemployment. His main emphasis, however, was on the supply side of the economy. The depression, he wrote, had come about because,

> It was nobody's business to ask 'What will be the social consequences of the action I propose to take? . . . Britain found herself unable to march to any one tune. With whatever good intentions, every regiment, indeed . . . every private soldier in the economic army started marching to his own tune. The result was discordance, disharmony and confusion.[9]

So far from being the ally of efficiency, in other words, the invisible hand of free competition had become its enemy. The only remedy was economic planning; and in an *ad hoc*, unsystematic, piecemeal fashion, private industry had already drawn that moral and started to plan its own activities. But piecemeal, *ad hoc* planning industry by industry was not enough; the time had come to supplement it with comprehensive planning on the national level. To achieve this, Macmillan advocated public ownership of the mines, electricity and the Bank of England; state control of transport and foreign trade; and an elaborate scheme of national and sectoral planning, supervised by a National Economic Council, chaired by a Minister of Economics and representing the employers and trades unions, as well as the government, the proposed foreign trade organisation and the Bank of England.[10]

While Macmillan was moving towards the mixed economy from the Right, some of his New Fabian contemporaries were moving towards it from the Left; The most notable was Evan Durbin, who published *The Politics of Democratic Socialism* in 1940. As the title implies, Durbin's scope was wide; the most interesting chapters in his book are concerned with the emotional roots of aggression and totalitarianism, and have little to do with economics. In his economic chapters, however, he set out a subtle and complicated case for combining economic planning with the price mechanism. Between them, he argued, the rise of the trades unions, the expansion of the social services, progressive taxation and depression-induced regulation of output in hard-hit sectors of the economy had choked the free play of the market and endangered saving. As a result, competitive capitalism could no longer function properly. But there was no point in trying to sweep away the restrictions and rigidities which frustrated free competition; they were the products of popular pressures, inevitable in a democracy, and could be eliminated only by suspending democracy. Only planning could correct the failures of the strangulated, monopolistic capitalism which had replaced the competitive capitalism of the past; and planning required the nationalisation of 'some considerable but limited section of the industrial system', together with the creation of a supreme economic authority to plan the socialised sector. But the private sector would still be much bigger than the public, and planning would operate through market pricing.[11] As his daughter has recently emphasised, Durbin was an egalitarian socialist, not a social liberal, still less a One Nation Conservative;[12] his ideal society would have been very different from Harold Macmillan's or even from that of the authors of the *Yellow Book*. Yet the political economy he envisaged had much more in common with theirs than with the command economy favoured on the left wing of his own party.

Albeit in different ways, Evan Durbin, Harold Macmillan and the authors of the *Yellow Book* all looked forward to a new kind of political economy, which did not exist at the time they wrote. Where they travelled hopefully, the fifth of the texts which deserve attention here – Anthony Crosland's *The Future of Socialism*, published in 1956 – celebrates the arrival. Thanks partly to the Keynesian revolution, and partly to the social and economic reforms of the wartime coalition and the post-war Labour government, Crosland argued, capitalism had been transformed – so much so that it was no longer clear that it still deserved the name. Because of this, socialism was no longer about the ownership of the means of production; it was not even about supply-side intervention of the sort discussed by Evan Durbin and other New Fabians fifteen years before. Instead, it was about the way to distribute the fiscal dividend of economic growth. Its distinguishing value was equality; and greater equality was to be achieved, partly through social and educational reforms, partly through redistributive taxation, particularly of inherited wealth, and partly by accepting 'an extremely high priority for the relief of social distress or misfortune, in contrast to the much lower priority which it would receive in a "free" economy guided mainly by an individualistic philosophy'.[13] To achieve all this, it was also necessary to achieve a high rate of economic growth – partly because rising living standards were themselves egalitarian in effect, and partly because there was no hope of winning public support for redistribution without it. But although rapid growth was essential, there was no need to 'strain every nerve to get the maximum rate of growth at almost any cost':[14] the existing growth rate was enough to double the standard of living in twenty-five years, and there was no need to worry if other economies grew faster still. Nor was there any need for detailed state intervention in the supply-side of the economy; Keynesian demand management would do the trick. With *The Future of Socialism*, then, the progressive tradition had come full circle. Like Hobhouse's before the First World War, Crosland's were the politics of equitable consumption: one of his most fundamental assumptions is that, in the new, post-Keynesian, post-capitalist era, production could safely be left to take care of itself.

III

Rarely has authoritative prophecy been so thoroughly belied. A decade after *The Future of Socialism* was published, its author was a minister in a government dogged, throughout its term of office, by the effects of sluggish growth and declining competitiveness. A decade after that, an even less fortunate government, of which he was an even more prominent member, had to make the most swingeing public-expenditure cuts of the post-war period so as to obtain the IMF credits to halt what one of its Treasury permanent secretaries was later to call a 'free fall' of the currency.[15]

Croslandite revisionism was not, however, the only victim of the storms of the 1960s and 1970s. The other versions of the progressive tradition fared no better. The post-war consensus falls naturally into three phases. In the first phase, which lasted until the late 1940s, an only partially demobilised economy was controlled in detail from Whitehall. In the second phase – which might be called the arm's length phase, and which lasted until the early 1960s – governments relied almost entirely on the Keynesian manipulation of demand, leaving the supply-side of the economy to its own devices. The third phase – best described, perhaps, as the hands-on phase – began with the Macmillan government's conversion to a formal incomes policy and indicative economic planning in 1960-2, and died away during the long diminuendo of the Callaghan government from 1976 to 1979. In that phase, governments of both parties supplemented Keynesian demand management with a bewildering variety of interventions in the supply-side, all springing from the tacit assumption that production could not be left to take care of itself after all. And in spirit – indeed, in some cases even in the letter – the interventionism practised by the 'hands-on' governments of the 1960s and 1970s was extraordinarily close to that advocated by the progressives of the 1920s and 1930s. If Croslandite revisionism failed to halt the secular decline of the British economy, so did the social liberalism of the *Yellow Book*, the social conservatism of *The Middle Way* and the reformist Fabianism of *The Politics of Democratic Socialism*.

Why did they fail? As we have seen, the *simpliste* answer that the policies they generated were doomed from the start does not stand up to serious investigation: in other countries, similar policies succeeded. The true answer must therefore lie deeper. It lies, I believe, less in what the progressives said than in what they failed to say: less in their answers to the questions which concerned them than in the questions they did not bother to ask: less in their explicit arguments than in the implicit assumptions which they saw no reason to examine.

These assumptions had to do, above all, with the role and structure of the state, and with the relationship between the British state and other states. As I have tried to show, the progressive tradition was a child of the late-nineteenth and early-twentieth centuries. That is, of course, another way of saying that it was a child of the generation between the third Reform Act and the First World War: of the period, in other words, when the Westminster model of parliamentary democracy took its modern form. It is hardly surprising that the progressives of later periods should have seen that model, and its underlying conventions and assumptions, as the embodiment of their political ideal: after all, their intellectual ancestors had formulated the theories which legitimised it, while their political ancestors had fought, often against fierce opposition, to bring it into being. Thus, while there were differences within the progressive camp about some of the model's incidental details – in the inter-war period, at any rate, Social Liberals were usually in favour of proportional representation, while New Fabians and One Nation Conservatives were mostly content with the traditional first-past-the-post system which most other European democracies had by now abandoned – all progressives were committed, usually without exploring the implications, to the central core. All took for granted the fundamental Westminster doctrines of individual and collective ministerial responsibility and the even more fundamental doctrine of absolute and inalienable parliamentary sovereignty. All assumed thereby that state power was inherently unshareable: that the power was, and should be, wielded only by national ministers responsible to the national parliament: and that the processes of democratic election and parliamentary scrutiny provided adequate safeguards against its abuse. More remarkably, all also assumed that, no matter what new functions the state acquired or what new developments took place in the world beyond its frontiers, the model would continue to work as well in the future as it had done in the past.

The result was a paradox, or rather a series of paradoxes. One of the central assumptions of the progressive tradition was that, in certain spheres at any rate, public power should redress the balance of the market. Almost by definition, then, progressive policies entailed an enormous expansion in the role, functions and complexity of government. Hobhouse's social liberalism laid the foundations for the welfare state, on which Beveridge and the post-war Labour government later erected the structure we know today.

The supply-side interventionism foreshadowed by Harold Macmillan, Evan Durbin and the authors of the *Yellow Book* implied, not only a welfare state, but an entrepreneurial or developmental state, intruding in a host of ways into the economic lives of its citizens. The enlarged and active state which all this was bound to bring into being was a quite different animal from the unobtrusive fledgling of the late nineteenth century. It took its decisions in different ways; it related to the citizen in different ways; it was subject to different pressures and different constraints; the politicians who presided over it had to satisfy a different kind of electorate, with different expectations and different values. For all these reasons, it could not behave as the state of the Westminster model was supposed to behave. But because the founding fathers of the progressive tradition had taken the model for granted, they had not foreseen the full implications of these differences; and when the new, progressive state actually arrived on the scene after the Second World War, their intellectual descendants behaved as though it were merely the old, Westminster state writ large. And because the progressives of the post-war period did not understand the true nature of the animal they were trying to ride, they did not ride it successfully.

Two examples must suffice. The fundamental Westminster doctrine of absolute and inalienable parliamentary sovereignty logically implies that the Crown-in-Parliament – the embodiment of the British state – cannot share power with either subnational or supranational tiers of government. But we live in an interdependent world, in which no medium-sized European nation state is effectively sovereign in foreign, defence or macro-economic policy. In such a world, no single West European government is, or is ever again likely to be, master in its own economic house. The notion of Keynesianism in one country is now as fantastic as the old Stalinist notion of socialism in one country. As the Wilson-Callaghan government discovered in the 1970s, and the Mitterrand government in the 1980s, unilateral Keynesianism in a world which has turned its back on Keynes is a recipe for inflation, balance-of-payments deficits and currency depreciation, not for full employment. The implications go further than appears at first sight. The central progressive project of using public power to redress the balance of the market can no longer be accomplished on the level of the classical nation-state alone. It must either be abandoned – the moral drawn by the New Right – or pursued on the supra-national level as well. But it cannot be pursued on the supra-national level unless national governments share power with the appropriate supra-national institutions – in the case of European governments, with the institutions of the EEC. And, until recently at any rate, only a minority, even among progressives, accepted the full implications of that conclusion.

The second example is more controversial. Not only do we live in an interdependent world, we also live in an interdependent society, dense with organised and unorganised groups, whose willing co-operation in the productive process is essential to the health of the economy. By virtue of the economic functions of their members, these groups can frustrate the policies of elected governments: whether parliamentary politicians like it or not, they too have broken the Westminster monopoly of effective sovereignty. Where international interdependence logically implies power-sharing between the national and supra-national tiers of government, social interdependence implies power-sharing between public authorities and a variety of organised groups of producers. But the doctrines and assumptions of Westminster parliamentarianism rule out the second as well as the first. In practice, of course, the progressive governments of the post-war era had to share power with the producer groups; indeed, there is some evidence that British governments were beginning to do this even between the wars.[16] But they did so covertly rather than openly, through inexplicit, fluctuating conventions and tacit understandings, not through clearly defined and generally known procedures. When negotiations took place between government and the producer groups, the general public had no way of knowing what the groups were asking for or what concessions they were prepared to make. Since the producer groups did not have to justify themselves in public, they faced no public pressure to reconcile incompatible claims or to accommodate themselves to the general interest. The whole system was at once unaccountable, apologetic and unstable – a perfect recipe for protectionist collusion against the public interest; and a perfect recipe, also, for ill-tempered breakdowns amid accusations of bad faith.

It is perhaps inevitable that, in a nation dogged by economic failure, public debate should focus almost exlusively on economic issues. Yet, if the argument set out here is right, this focus is misplaced. The symptoms of Britain's ills may be economic, but the causes are political. Politics, not economics, brought the post-war consensus to grief; the shortcomings of the tradition on which it was based sprang from failures of political imagination, not from failures of economic analysis. The revival of the tradition depends on its ability to put those political failures right.

DISCUSSION ON TWO

In discussion, considerable doubts were expressed about the coherence of the progressive tradition; to increase planning indefinitely without changing the system of government was an intellectual fudge. Being against unemployment and for growth were not ideologically contentious but beyond that the 'middle way' always fell apart on the issue of efficiency, which invariably sorted out the egalitarians from the inegalitarians and pushed people back towards Left or Right. When the going became tough, a widening gap developed between progressive parties as to both ends and means.

David Marquand agreed that there was a certain amount of posturing by Labour revisionists, whose explicit egalitarianism was a way of saying: 'Look, chaps, I'm still really a socialist.' Crosland was tortured by the need to rein back public expenditure after the IMF imposed their conditions in 1976. Hard questions of equality always tended to drift back into equality of opportunity. Here it was suggested that the SDP's commitment to a 'more equal' society was also a fudge. What was the criterion of more equality? And what had the rather incoherent progressive tradition to teach social democracy?

David Marquand responded that he had not set out to defend it but to define it – and perhaps it was not as incoherent as all that: both Conservative equality of opportunity and Labour equality had been plugged into the same brand of corporate capitalism. The progressive collapse of this from the early seventies now posed the need for new institutional arrangements within which agreement could be secured. It was pointed out that SDP and Liberals alike attached great importance to institutional change; at the heart of David Marquand's analysis of the ultimate failure of the 'middle way' in Britain lay the refusal of either of the major parties to contemplate any modification whatsoever of the Westminster model and the continuing belief of both Conservatives and Labour that state power was inherently unshareable either at a higher or a lower level. This critique of Westminster commanded general consent but a warning note was uttered against over-dependence on the magical powers of institutional reform without a matching change in behaviour patterns. The National Economic Development Office

(NEDO) already existed but was ineffectual through lack of political will to make it work.

Attention also focused (once again) on the surprising degree of intervention in the economy advocated by the Liberals of the inter-war period. This, it was suggested, was motivated partly by the view that the individual could no longer swim without state aid against the strong tides of advanced capitalism and by the belief shared by all progressive parties that the 'invisible hand' of classical economics no longer worked as it was supposed to work and therefore investment could not be left to market forces alone.

The response to David Marquand's paper was lively but somewhat diffuse. A number of important topics had emerged, which it was agreed would have to be tackled in subsequent sessions, not least the questions of how much equality and how much institutional reform are desirable. However, despite their other differences, all the components of the progressive tradition were at least agreed on one thing, namely the collapse of the 'invisible hand'. It was therefore agreed that we should first make an excursion further back in time and set Adam Smith in perspective, if only because he was so constantly prayed in aid by the New Right and indeed elevated by them to the rank of patron saint. Also, in the very first discussion of the group on the empirical tradition it had been urged that the Adam Smith Institute and the Institute of Economic Affairs should not be allowed to get away with only one side of Smith – *The Wealth of Nations* – without acknowledging the other, represented by *The Theory of Moral Sentiments*. George Goyder, well versed in Smith, offered to prepare a paper.

THREE

The Real Adam Smith
From *The Theory of Moral Sentiments* to *The Wealth of Nations*

GEORGE GOYDER

(1) Benevolence

Adam Smith's aim in *The Wealth of Nations* is to unlock the secret of national prosperity. Economics is, for Smith, a branch of philosophy, and the object of philosophy is to determine 'wherein consisted the happiness and perfection of a man, considered not only as an individual, but as the member of a family, of a state, and of the great society of mankind'.[1]

Adam Smith's view of human nature is optimistic. Like Hutcheson, his predecessor in the chair of moral philosophy at the University of Glasgow, Smith was influenced by the Earl of Shaftesbury's *Characteristicks* (1711), which combined morals with aesthetics in an equation which ran along the lines: beauty equals truth, truth order, order sociability, sociability morality. Smith takes sociability as his starting point, together with the love of approbation, for his *Theory of Moral Sentiments* (1759). 'All the members of human society stand in need of each other's assistance and are likewise exposed to mutual injuries. Where the necessary assistance is reciprocally afforded from love, from gratitude, from friendship and esteem, the society flourishes and is happy.'[2]

(2) Justice and Utility

But human society does not only depend upon the mutual benevolence of its members. It can continue to hold together from the sense of utility or self-interest, so long as the rules of justice are observed. The moment injury begins, however, the bonds which bind society together are broken. 'Society may subsist, tho' not in the most comfortable state, without beneficence; but the prevalence of injustice must utterly destroy it'.[3] One is reminded of the dictum of Montesquieu, in *L'Esprit des Lois,* that the survival of democracy depends on virtue in the citizen.[4]

The chapter heading of Part IV of *The Theory of Moral Sentiments* is 'Of the Effect of Utility upon the Sentiment of Approbation'. Here Smith paints an amusing picture of the vanity, ostentation, and love of approbation of the human race. The householder who is constantly re-arranging his furniture, instead of sitting down; the dandy who claims his watch is accurate to the second, but is himself invariably late, are types of that human egoism that demands means, and ever more means, rather than ends. Their demands and ambitions are, however, what makes the world go round.

(3) The Invisible Hand

This is the point at which the invisible hand makes its appearance – Smith's most pregnant and famous expression. After describing the process by which individual demands are translated into collective prosperity, Smith writes: 'The rich . . . are led by an invisible hand to make nearly the same distribution of the necessaries of life which would have been made, had the earth been divided into equal portions among all its inhabitants, and thus without intending it, without knowing it, advance the interest of the society.'[5]

Every individual, says Smith, is continually exerting himself to find out the most advantageous employment of whatever capital he can command. This leads him to prefer the employment which is most advantageous to society. But justice remains the final criterion of economic policy. 'The establishment of perfect justice, of perfect liberty, and of perfect equality, is the very simple secret which most effectually secures the highest degree of prosperity.'[6]

We must remember that when Smith was writing, the Industrial Revolution had hardly begun. Britain was still a nation of small workshops, each commonly employing fewer than a dozen people. The liability of the family-owned business was unlimited, and failure could mean disaster. It was to be another hundred years (1862) before the introduction of limited liability, which Arthur Bryant describes as being the most influential measure ever to have been passed by a British parliament.[7].

The family-dominated business system of 1776 was very different from today, when a hundred large firms produce one half of Britain's manufactures. It is because the individual proprietor, or entrepreneur, in Smith's day was a member of a local community and a product of the local social environment, that he could be left in general to pursue his own interest. Smith believed that for the economy to flourish, a balance needed to be kept and that this balance, or equilibrium, was more likely to be achieved through a large number of separate individual decisions than by any kind of central direction. The free working of the competitive price mechanism was the best way to maximise resource allocation and employment, and the assumption of full employment explains the key role accorded to resource allocation via the market.

(4) The Theory of Equilibrium

What Smith regards as a tendency in *The Theory of Moral Sentiments* becomes a law in *The Wealth of Nations*. 'It is only for the sake of profit that any man employs a capital in support of industry; and he will always therefore endeavour to employ it in the support of that industry of which the produce is likely to be of the greatest value . . . he intends only his own gain, and he is in this, as in many other cases, led by an invisible hand to promote an end which was no part of his intention.'[8]

Although believing the invisible hand to be the most dependable regulator of economic equilibrium, Smith is well aware that, left to itself, the balance between utility and justice will be upset. As it turns out, the equilibrium theory requires the intervention of government at a surprisingly large number of points. Smith requires four main reforms: free trade, free exports and imports, free choice of occupation, and free trade in land. All this is over and above the natural duties of government, which for Smith comprised defence, order, justice, education and public works. In Smith's view the government should control monopolies and tax them heavily, the gains of monopolists being 'of all subjects the most proper' [for taxation].[9] Duties and prohibitions on trade should be removed along with laws of succession and apprenticeship which artificially restrict the market for land and skilled labour. Wherever there is an exclusive corporation it may be proper to regulate prices. Smith also recognised the danger of a corrupt or incompetent government being worse than the evils of unrestrained selfishness. In this Smith is a realist; he neither despises government nor idealises it.

(5) The Limits of Government Intervention

Smith recognised that conflict might arise in at least six areas: in wage bargaining, in the relations of manufacturers and consumers, between landlords and the public, from price rings, from too much speculative investment, and from neglect of communications. Government must be prepared to regulate and interfere in all these spheres since the maintainance of justice is essential. 'The modern advocate of *laissez-faire* who objects to government participation in business on the ground that it is an encroachment upon a field reserved by nature for private enterprise cannot find any support for this argument in *The Wealth Of Nations'* (Jacob Viner).[10] More surprisingly, Smith would require government to regulate the rate of interest. He endorses the statutory rate of 5% as the maximum that should be permitted. At the time Smith was writing public credit stood at 3%, the statutory limit having been reduced in 1714 from 8% to 5%. Anything higher than 5% would, in Smith's view, encourage 'prodigals and projectors' with the result that 'a great part of the capital of the country would thus be kept out of the hands which were most likely to make a profitable and advantageous use of it.'[11] Smith wished to discourage investment of a speculative character abroad, in the interest of investment at home that would enable domestic employment to be maintained. In seeking to limit the rate of interest, Smith was being inconsistent, as Jeremy Bentham hastened to point out in his *Defence of Usury* (1787).

But it is precisely Smith's inconsistency at this point which reveals the philosopher dominating the economist. Smith is well aware of the long-standing tradition that the pursuit of money for its own sake distorts the economy and must be controlled if there is to be economic equilibrium. Maynard Keynes shows the same awareness in the *General Theory* when he writes: 'For centuries, indeed for several milleniums, enlightened opinion held for certain and obvious a doctrine which the classical school has repudiated . . . I mean the doctrine that the rate of interest . . . constantly tends to rise too high, so that a wise government is concerned to curb it by statute and custom and even by invoking the sanctions of the moral law'.[12]

In seeking to moderate interest rates, Smith is treading in the tradition of Aristotle as interpreted by the Christian church. The doctrine of usury, as R.H. Tawney points out, in *A Discourse Upon Usury*,[13] was an attempt to regulate the price of money so as to achieve equilibrium between borrower and lender. Adam Smith was well aware of this tradition and appears to subscribe to it. This would explain his remark that 'the rate of profit . . . is always highest in the countries which are going fastest to ruin'.[14]

(6) The Supply of Capital

The reason for Smith's concern with 'prodigals and projectors' is that he believes 'the general industry of society never can exceed what the capital of the society can employ'.[15] The increase in the quantity of useful labour actually employed within any society must depend altogether upon the capital which employs it.[16] The accumulation of capital is the natural result of the economies brought about by the increasing division of labour, and by the urge to save. Smith looks to the savings of ordinary people to supply the capital needed to employ the available work force. Given a free market for labour and capital, there should be no unemployment, except that which arises from the need for temporary structural and cyclical adjustment. But a free market is essential. Mercantilism, which we call protection, favoured joint stock companies created by parliament or by royal charter, put restrictions on trade, created artificial obstacles to a free labour market, and encouraged cosy price-fixing devices, all of which should be abolished, if there were to be economic equilibrium and full employment.

(7) The Control of Monopoly

Monopoly in all its forms is anathema to Smith, not only because it acts against the interests of the consumer, but because it distorts 'that natural proportion which would otherwise establish itself between judicious industry and profit'. Consumption being the sole end and purpose of all production, the interest of the producer ought to be attended to 'only so far as may be necessary for promoting that of the consumer'. Smith regards this proposition as so self-evident as to make it 'absurd to attempt to prove it'.[17]

Monopoly in Adam Smith's day was conferred by the state granting an exclusive privilege to a trading corporation, either at home or abroad. What in Smith's time were known as regulated or joint stock companies, are today represented by public companies. The antagonism of Smith to monopoly in all its forms would surely apply to the huge concerns which today dominate the market. Nor is Smith particularly sympathetic towards the commercial community. He speaks of their 'mean rapacity and monopolising spirit' and denies that they are or ought to be 'the rulers of mankind'.[18] In the light of his theory of equilibrium, we may conclude that Smith would have questioned the takeover bid as a means of increasing a company's already large share of the market. Nor would the pursuit by pension fund managers of short-term profits through supporting a takeover have appealed to Smith. It is tempting to speculate on the remedy he would have proposed to the massive growth of corporate power in our time. Would Smith have sought to give the consumers and workers some rights within the large firm, such as the right to be heard, or the right of the worker to be a member of the company? The alternative of splitting up large concerns would hardly seem practical as a general rule.

(8) The Division of Labour

The Wealth of Nations begins with a discussion of the economic advantages of the division of labour and the increased efficiency it generates. 'The greatest improvement in the productive powers of labour, and the greater part of the skill, dexterity and judgment with which it is anywhere directed, or applied, seems to have been the effect of the division of labour.'[19] 'It is the great multiplication of the productions of all the different arts, in consequence of the division of labour, which occasions, in a well governed society, that universal opulence which extends itself to the lowest ranks of the people'.[20]

There is, however, another side to the benefits to be reaped from the divison of labour and Smith shows himself well aware of its dangers. Smith is discussing the education of women, which he claims is excellent, precisely because, unlike the education of men, 'every part of their education tends evidently to some useful purpose.'[21] He goes on to advocate government action to prevent 'the almost entire corruption and degeneracy of the great body of the people.'[22] To what does Smith attribute this liability to corruption? To the division of labour and its effects. Here Smith the economist gives way to Smith the sociologist and the philosopher. Smith is peering into the future and does not like what he sees. This is what he writes:

> In the progress of the division of labour, the employment of the far greater part of those who live by labour . . . comes to be confined to a very few simple operations, frequently to one or two. The man whose life is spent in performing a few simple operations, of which the effects too are perhaps always the same, or very nearly the same, has no occasion to exert his understanding or to exercise his invention in finding out expedients for removing difficulties which never occur. He naturally loses, therefore, the habit of such exertion, and generally becomes as stupid

and ignorant as it is possible for a human being to become. The torpor of his mind renders him not only incapable of relishing or bearing a part in any rational conversation, but of conceiving any generous, noble or tender sentiment, and consequently of forming any just judgement concerning many even of the ordinary duties of private life. Of the great and extensive interests of his country he is altogether incapable of judging.[23]

This account of the human effects of industrialisation may seen overdrawn. But it shows an aspect of Adam Smith's mind that goes well beyond the power of economic analysis. As Sir Henry Phelps Brown has put it: 'Smith's gift of empathy, his power of entering imaginatively into the workings of human nature, make him an instructive guide to our own world of labour.'[24] Smith's remedy was to create parish schools where the children would at least learn to read, write and account, and receive some technical training. Today this is accepted state policy. But there remains a sense of alienation on the part of the worker that has still to be overcome if prosperity in Britain is to prevail over decline. Smith would have been scathing about some of the monopolistic practices of trades unions. But he would also have wished to identify the worker more closely with his work and workplace, with a view to recovering that state of equilibrium in which self-interest and benevolence can be reconciled through the application of justice.

(9) The Supply of Entrepreneurs

It is tempting to quote Smith in aid of one's own economic nostrums. One thing is certain; Smith was no *laissez-faire* man. He sought justice and believed in the operation of market forces. Where monopoly prevailed, Smith would have government act to recreate the market.

As Smith is at pains to emphasise, there can be no employment without a prior stock of capital. Smith's theory of the market assumes a willing lender meeting a willing worker and agreeing on terms. The theory corresponded reasonably closely to the fact in Smith's day when industry was local, labour relatively unorganised and immobile, and the banks in close touch with their customers. This was, according to Smith, especially true in Scotland, where the local bank manager would chivy his customers regularly for some repayment of the bank's loan, and if there was no reply, visit the borrower to find out if anything was wrong. It was relatively easy, in these conditions, for the banker to be able to distinguish the enterprise that was credit-worthy.

Today, it is all very different. The banks are highly centralised. If there is a serious local problem, the local banker is told to go upwards for advice and this means moving away from the local situation. The entrepreneur may be faced with a demand to mortgage his home. This puts him in the moral dilemma of sacrificing his family in order to create a venture. Since existing companies enjoy limited liability, why, Adam Smith might ask, discriminate against the very class of person on whom the future so largely depends for fresh employment and prosperity? Surely the clearing banks, with their profits of five hundred to one thousand million pounds each, can find some better way of protecting themselves, even if it means taking part of the equity? If we are to overcome mass unemployment we must somehow lower the price of capital. In non-inflationary terms Smith's upper limit of 5% would still seem right for new ventures. The price of labour also needs to become more market-orientated and this requires changes in the attitude of trades unions. But the creation of fresh enterprise concerns not only the price of capital and of labour. It concerns the company. A company like GEC, with surplus assets of over a billion pounds, might well be required to lend half that sum to a national enterprise board for the purpose of creating new businesses and encouraging local employment.

There is no shortage in Britain today of either labour or of capital. What is in short supply is the spirit of enterprise. We have taken the supply of entrepreneurs for granted, with the result that we have brought ourselves into a deep state of depression. Adam Smith with his usual perspicacity, foresaw this possibility:

> It is in the progressive state, while the society is advancing to the further acquisition, rather than when it has acquired its full complement of riches, that the condition of the labouring poor, of the great body of the people, seems to be the happiest and the most comfortable. It is hard in the stationary, and miserable in the declining state. The progressive state is in reality the cheerful and the hearty state to all the different orders of the society. The stationary is dull; the declining melancholy.[25]

In *The Wealth of Nations* the real Adam Smith combines the pursuit of wealth with common sense, humanity, and a constant regard for justice and we could do worse than to imitate him.

In the discussion on George Goyder's paper it was accepted that *The Wealth of Nations* had been conceived as part of a grander plan, in which *The Theory of Moral Sentiments* also played an important part. But mutuality, approbation, approval by one's fellows in a small-scale production society belonged – it was suggested – to an optimistic view of the world that had not been borne out in practice. Smith, certainly, aimed at equilibrium but this depended on a balance between *efficiency,* to be obtained by the suspension of monopolies, and *sympathy,* which descended from Shaftesbury's concept of *benevolence.* Once (monopolistic) mercantilism was defeated you got efficiency but the other half of the eighteenth-century equation represented by *sympathy/benevolence* was jettisoned. Smith and his contemporaries no doubt felt it would be kept on board but it was not.

On these grounds and on others – that his labour theory of value and his linkage of population growth with prosperity were both plain wrong – it was argued by some that Smith was no longer relevant, was at best 'a great man, a great read'. On the other hand, the labour theory of value is still the basis of Marxism and of socialism, both of which are still alive. Also, George Goyder was able to argue with conviction and to some effect that though Smith's economic model might be out of date, he would certainly have disapproved of the great concentrations of economic power in the modern world and in particular of takeover mania and excessive speculation – and that these were also valid concerns for contemporary social democrats. Smith would not, according to George Goyder, have interpreted *laissez-faire* as supporting massive producer interests against the consumer. It was also pointed out that, though Smith was always quoted in Britain as the apostle of *laissez-faire,* he was not the father of the doctrine; the earlier version of the phrase *'laissez-nous faire'* was first addressed by the merchants of Lyons to Colbert and was coined in response to the quite different circumstances of the suffocating state power of the French *ancien régime.*

As a result of this discussion it was agreed that a cardinal issue for social democracy was how to control the great monolithic corporations which have grown up in this century and which Smith in his wildest dreams could not have foreseen. It was also clear that, though utility might seem a common coin first minted in the eighteenth century, neither Smith nor Hume, owing to their attachment respectively to sympathy and to benevolence, was in any modern sense a utilitarian; neither was interested in a rational calculus for measuring happiness. As Benthamite utilitarianism and classical liberalism are so intimately linked, the next step seemed to be to invite an expert on utilitarianism to talk to us. Alan Ryan agreed to do this.

FOUR

Utilitarianism from Philosophical Radicalism to Social Democracy

ALAN RYAN

John Stuart Mill's impact on utilitarian moral and political theory has been described in many places and in many ways. As early as the 1830s his former friend and confidant J.A. Roebuck remarked that Mill had begun by being a logician and economist, but then he had read Wordsworth and had become terribly muddled. Twentieth-century commentators have been in several minds as to whether he remained a utilitarian in a somewhat stretched sense, 'really' abandoned utilitarianism for an eclectic liberalism, or rather saw for the first time what the full resources of utilitarianism were and how they might be deployed. I have elsewhere joined in these debates and will not waste the reader's time by doing so here.[1] For there is another aspect to the history of Mill's transformation of his 'Benthamite' inheritance which is equally interesting and less discussed; this is his transformation of utilitarian politics from the politics of philosophical radicalism to the politics of social democracy.

I tackle this topic thematically rather than historically, both because the history of philosophical radicalism has already been treated by abler hands than mine, and because my intentions here are at least partly polemical and better served by a more schematic approach. Mill's intellectual situation in, say, 1850 was not unlike that of the impatient but chastened reformer of today. The manual working classes – then, of course, a much larger proportion of the population than now – had alternated between sullen acquiescence in the existing order, enthusiastic support of that order when stirred by jingoistic leaders, and hopelessly ambitious attempts at insurrection. What they had never achieved was steady, controlled progress towards genuine self-government. Yet Mill knew – or thought he knew – that in the long run nothing would work save something best described as social democracy, and that it would not work until the working classes understood its merits and were willing to practise the self-control and learn the skills it demanded of them.[2] To get this to happen needed a change of mind and a change of heart both in the working class and in the middle and upper class, for the latter had to acquiesce in the transfer of at any rate some of their power to their social, political and economic inferiors. The political leadership which would promote the steady growth of social democracy was, however, hard to see. Mill's attitude to the political leaders of his day is hard to summarise, but it is fair to say that he was at any rate sceptical of the aristocracy as a class, even if he briefly thought that Lord Durham might be the saving of the radicals. His great chapter on 'The Probable Futurity of the Labouring Classes' in the *Principles of Political Economy* makes it clear that he thought it morally obnoxious and socially impossible to try to govern the working class from above – Disraelian ideals of a responsible aristocracy and a deferential and grateful populace struck no chords in his heart. Nor for that matter did Carlyle's version of the theory of leadership; neither Abbot Sampson nor Frederick the Great appealed to Mill as a recipe for everyday politics.

In later life, Mill did his best to promote the careers of working-class leaders such as Odger, Appleyard and Holyoake; he tried to persuade Liberal constituencies to adopt them as their candidates in parliamentary elections and argued that the lack of working-class representation in parliament was a considerable weakness. His reasons were very much his own. He did not think that middle- and upper-class Liberals were hostile or indifferent to working-class interests; if anything, he wrote, they were inclined to be too friendly to them. What other classes inevitably lacked was the vivid sense of what those interests were which members of the class possessed. It was a representative function which only they could perform. The same argument obviously applied to women and to almost any other distinct legitimate interest. But what is quite clear is that Mill realised that there was a problem about the politics of the nineteenth century to which Bentham and the philosophical radicals had supplied no answer – or, rather, there were two problems, one a matter of ideals, the other a matter of political practice. It must, I think, be admitted that Mill was more impressive as a preacher of the ideals than as a practitioner of the politics of their realisation, though even there he was by no means inept.

The philosophical radicals were a much more mixed group than their name suggests, or, to put it somewhat differently, fewer of the radicals of 1780-1840 are properly called 'philosophical' radicals than Mill suggests. It may well have been Mill who began the tradition of regarding Bentham as the brains and James Mill as the organising genius of radicalism; it was certainly Halévy who cemented the idea with the famous dictum that 'Bentham gave [James] Mill a doctrine and Mill gave Bentham a school'.[3] Though well said, it is at best a half truth. The union of anti-Tory forces which eventually pushed through Catholic Emancipation, the repeal of the Toleration Act, and the first Reform Act was much like all other coalitions – dissenters lined up with utilitarian agnostics when it suited them (as it very often did), Whigs who thought it high time they regained office flirted with plebeian radicals in seats where the franchise was wide enough to make it plausible, disciples of Cobbett who were sick of corruption allied themselves with theorists of cheap government whom Cobbett habitually dismissed as 'feelosophical villains'.

Mill grew up as the white hope of the utilitarian wing of radicalism; not, however as its white hope for political leadership, rather as its intellectual leader. In his own eyes at least he inherited the duty to promote a Bentham-inspired programme of reform in law, political representation, and education; the emotional breakdown in the winter of 1826-7 that succeeded the extraordinary education chronicled in his *Autobiography* persuaded him that pure Benthamism would not do as the foundation of either social or individual happiness. In explaining both to himself and his wider readership just why it would not do, he developed his own distinctive brand of liberalism or, as we might well call it, social democracy with a liberal face. The foundations of Benthamism, he thought, were laid in an analytical frame of mind which held that all social reform must be prefaced by an inquest into why existing behaviour, belief and institutions were, or were not, utilitarianly efficient. This was all to the good; but it was not enough. For individuals in particular, it was necessary to cultivate the emotions as well as to analyse them. Poetry, music and painting all had their place; many desires and ambitions did not need analysis so much as encouragement – a sense of honour, individual dignity, the urge to make one's mark on the world – these were the sort of thing Bentham had chronically neglected in favour of narrowly self-interested and calculating reactions, and to leave them out was to leave out most of what made life valuable and human character admirable. We do not need to inquire how far this was fair to Bentham. It may have been unfair to the private person, but it was not unfair to the public image which Bentham cultivated and which the *Westminster Review* had cultivated too.[4]

What is worth discussing is what the shift meant for Mill's liberalism. Bentham was not above all else a liberal; he did not believe that the preservation and enhancement of freedom was a coherent goal of government, did not believe in any 'natural right' to liberty, and was insistent that government involved the curtailment of freedom for the sake of other goods such as security and prosperity. The question is whether he was really contemptuous of liberty, too, or merely eager to make his readers understand that liberty is something other than security or property or self-government. Some critics have dwelt at length on the liberticide quality of Bentham's famous Panopticon, his design for a prison in which the jailer could see all his prisoners at all times without being seen by them and could exercise a benign but complete discipline dreamed of by nobody before Bentham.[5] This 'mill for grinding rogues honest' was capable of being used as prison, infirmary or workhouse and was much denounced as a symbol of Bentham's intention to fetter the poor with middle-class supervision and cover the country with parallelograms of paupers. Bentham affected not to understand the complaint; he thought it merely sentimental to complain at a machine which, if it worked, would protect society and reform the criminal, and do it cheaply. In a foretaste of 1980s free-market thinking, he pointed out that the Panopticon system could make a decent profit if the prisons were let out to entrepreneurs who could use their charges' labour. But Bentham was not a foe to freedom. He was an inspiration to the liberators of Spanish America and to the radicals of the Iberian peninsula itself; he was violently opposed to slavery; he was an advocate of universal suffrage and votes for women. He thought that governments were ill-advised to meddle with the private convictions of their subjects and was therefore hostile to legislation on sexual or religious issues; the harmless private enjoyments which most people wished to have secured to them were a matter of indifference to government, which should concentrate on protecting the competent as they went about their business and on rescuing the maladroit or unlucky if they came unstuck, i.e. one got a great deal of *de facto* liberalism out of Bentham, even if he was hostile to constitutionalism, to doctrines of natural right, and to old-fashioned ideas about the freedom enjoyed by the ancient republics.[6]

Oddly, Mill turns all this right round. Because Mill so extended the range of goods which we might care for, he extended the range of things a government might concern itself with. Some writers have seen in this clear evidence that Mill was less of a liberal than Bentham. Bentham thought that governments ought to let us alone unless there was some very pressing good to be gained by interference; Mill's moralising liberalism condemns 'let-alone' as a creed and seems to cast government – once government has fallen into the hands of middle-class progressives like himself – in the role of governess. It is true that what government is to teach us is self-respect, moral independence and the rest of it; nonetheless, anyone who does not much want to be preached at will find Mill's ideal government decidedly interfering. Bentham's vulgar claim that 'quantity of pleasure being equal, pushpin is as good as poetry' may be bad aesthetics, but it is good politics.[7] Even if this is an exaggeration – and it is – it contains the seed of an important thought and one we can extend. Mill insisted, *contra* Bentham and his father, that the very principles on which government ought to be constructed inevitably varied through time; what society needed at one epoch was different from what it needed at another. Good government was government adapted to and favourable to the moral growth of the particular society in question. Thus, Mill's *Representative Government* argues that no serious argument about politics can take place in the absence of a theory of history; we need to know the general pattern of moral and political progress before we know what kind of government we require. None the less, says Mill, there is one absolutely best kind of government even though it is defined in terms of progress rather than in simply utilitarian terms; representative government is uniquely fitted both to employ and extend the abilities of those who live under it. It makes more demands upon the citizenry than any other form of government, so it is only at a high level of general literacy and intelligence that representative government is possible; but, in making its citizens govern themselves, it encourages them to cultivate precisely those qualities they need – self-reliance, self-control, energy, wide interests, public spirit.[8]

In contrasting this conception of democracy with Bentham's view of politics we must briefly recur to our comparison of their attitudes to liberty. Mill is an interesting figure in the history of liberalism precisely because he does not argue for government abstention so much as for the creation of a positive enthusiasm for freedom among the entire population. Mill relies as much as Bentham on such utilitarian claims as that where interference is not visibly required for the maintenance of peace and good order, but only reflects public opinion on, say, sexual, racial or religious prejudice, it does no good and merely causes irritation and alienation, and ought to be refrained from for simple reasons of utility. Again, he accepts – though he does not make much of – the Benthamite claim that *laissez-faire* and economic freedom make for prosperity and growth and that most interference is ill-judged. It is, however, important to see that neither Mill nor Bentham takes the view that *laissez-faire* is forced upon us by the sanctity of property. A man's goods are 'his' only because the law says so; property is a social creation not a natural right, and the case for *laissez-faire* is instrumental rather than principled. The case for liberty in Mill's work, however, is principled through and through. That is, it is because liberty is both essential to the maintenance of other vitally important goods and is itself the principal ingredient in the happiness of any developed human life that Mill sets out to persuade his audience of the value of liberty. So Mill needs a good deal more than the observation that much interference does no good, and he duly provides it.

What he argues is that liberty is the chief element in the happiness of 'a man as a progressive being'.[9] Behind this lies an argument of the following sort: if we ask what the point is of coercion in human life, it is plain that its role, rationally considered, is to prevent aggression by one person upon another, and to some extent to reinforce elements of social co-operation without which life would be hopelessly insecure and miserable. It is this defence of minimal co-operation which accounts for Mill's certainty that we are entitled to force people to give evidence in a law court so that others will not suffer injustice, a case which is plainly different from merely forcing people not to attack one another. But we must now enquire what the main goods of life are. For Mill, they involve security as a basis, with the promotion of self-government and a capacity for the pursuit of ideals among the goals. So, the rules a society has to enforce, and back up by the coercion of law on the one hand and public opinion on the other, are rules which promote security, self-direction and openness. The enforcement of contracts plainly comes into this category; the enforcement of laws against assault or murder plainly do so; the provision of social facilities such as law courts do so.

Mill startles many of his modern readers when he insists that the same principles entitle society to demand that individuals exercise prudence in the breeding of children and impose upon every individual a duty to ensure that their children do not become a burden on society – it is not the exercise of my liberty to leave my offspring ignorant and incompetent, but a neglect of my duty to them and society at large. But Mill is unlike most casual thinkers about this subject in not thinking that marriage, producing children, securing their education are somehow 'private' or intimate matters which society ought not to interfere with. Mill's work is entirely barren of discussions of the realm of the private or intimate, which one might think a weakness, but which it would be a grave mistake to dismiss as an oversight. Mill's point is quite different; we must always ask whether social rules and social coercion would promote security and self-government – making people take care of their children is a legitimate act of self-defence, and it would be insane to suppose that children allowed to grow up ignorant and unemployable had much chance of practising self-government. By the same token, Mill's insistence on limiting the scope of rule-making and rule-enforcing was directed at precisely this target and was limited by just the historical considerations we glanced at above. Slavery was once a means to progress; it would be intolerable now, but we cannot exactly condemn it always and everywhere in the past. Despotism is a mode of government suitable for societies in the earliest stages of their progress towards universal self-government. Akbar, Peter the Great, Charlemagne, Elizabeth I are several times invoked as examples of benevolent despotism – or, perhaps, necessary-under-the-circumstances despotism. The rule of the East India Company was a more current example; Mill agreed that this distinguished institution governed India despotically in that it was unaccountable to those whom it ruled; but its aim, rationally considered, was not to subject Indians to Englishmen in perpetuity but to allow self-government to operate in India. As soon as Indians could govern themselves they should do so, and the East India Company should leave. (I don't suggest that Mill's view of the EIC was shared by many of its employees, let alone by its native subjects; all I want to point out is how Mill's liberalism finds itself forced to endorse compulsory liberation. It is often held to be a weakness of Marxism that it envisages people being forced to be free. It seems to me that liberalism is in just the same situation – either we have to allow people to enslave themselves on the grounds that they are free agents and must be left to do what they choose, or we bite the bullet and make them accept freedom.)

Now we must ask why Mill was so eager to press his notion of liberty on his readers, and the answer is that he had a vision of positive self-government in intellectual, moral, social and economic life which he thought could operate only if society took pains not to interfere with its members on paternalistic or moralising grounds. Many people find Mill's arguments for freedom of speech and opinion puzzling; they are quite right when they complain that the 'very simple principle' which Mill claims governs the argument of *Liberty* – the principle that we can only interfere with one another's liberty in self-defence – does not seem to explain the sanctity of free speech.[10] A good utilitarian might suppose that the question of just how free speech was to be was a matter of how much pleasure it gave people. Mill relies on something else; he relies on the idea that each of us either has, or would have once we had experienced it, a passionate desire to be his (or her) own man (or woman). Free speech is not so much about searching for the truth or allowing science to progress as about the basic idea that our ideas should be *our own*; the person who takes over the opinions of others has no need of anything but the 'ape-like faculty of imitation'. The progressive being to whom Mill directs the argument is a being committed to thinking for himself or herself. This appeal to the felt passion for freedom which makes those who feel it reject any amount of comfort in exchange for it is an appeal which Mill makes again at the end of his essay on 'The Subjection of Women'. He acknowledges that many men and many women too have argued that women do very well as they are; they are cared for by husbands, fathers or brothers and get a good bargain by exchanging their capacity to prettify existence for the paternalistic management of their affairs. He then asks his readers whether they accept this argument; would they go back to school, having left, would they return to the parental home, having set up on their own, would they support a government which sold national independence for prosperity? He assumes that they would answer no to all these questions and that they would thus condemn their defence of paternalism out of their own mouths.[11]

That brings us back to social democracy. For we can now see that what Mill adds to familiar utilitarian arguments for government answerability is a conception of freedom as self-government which extends the old doctrine both as moral theory and in its scope. Earlier forms of utilitarianism implied that *if* it had been possible to secure guaranteed benevolent, well-informed despotism there would have been nothing wrong with it. For the object of government is to promote the general interest at least cost, and benevolent despotism – in practice bureaucratic government – is the theoretically best route. It is because our rulers are always tempted to line their pockets from the public purse and promote their own interests rather than the public interest that we need some way of making them answerable to the public. This argument, essentially that of Bentham and James Mill, attaches no value to self-government for its own sake, and has no sympathy for the thought that some values are public and participatory rather than private. J.S. Mill held a wholly different view. For him, benevolent despotism was not merely impossible, it was wicked in principle; indeed, a benevolent despot might do more damage than a less benevolent despot would do, for the latter would arouse opposition, stir up people to act on their own behalf and inspire in them a desire to govern themselves, whereas the former might turn them into what de Tocqueville once described as 'industrious sheep'. Indeed, Mill's hostility to democracy as usually practised was precisely that it was prone to be a benevolent despotism; each of us is tyrannised over by everyone else, in a perfectly good-natured and benevolent fashion. Mill went back to classical ideals of citizenship for another view of democracy; individuals had to look outwards as well as inwards, they had to have public-spirited goals as well as private ones. They had to have some sense of their own ability to stand up for themselves and do so in public. For this reason Mill opposed the secret ballot; he was not in favour of mass meetings and crowd decisions, but he thought a self-respecting citizen ought to have the courage to tell the world what he or she had done with the vote. Voting isn't a 'private' act; when we vote for a member of parliament we are exercising power over our fellows, and they have a right to know how we have exercised that power, just as we have a duty to exercise it properly. It went without saying that anyone trying to intimidate a voter ought to be dealt with as savagely as any other malefactor; but, said Mill, a shade optimistically, while it had once been true that landlords and employers would have exerted improper pressures on the voter, now they could not do so. Accordingly, we should keep up the idea that the vote is a public duty by making people vote in public.[12]

The same arguments recur throughout *Representative Government;* the Athenians were cleverer, happier, more creative than any people in history because of their participatory political order. Modern man must serve on public bodies – jury service is an instance, but Mill envisaged people doing stints on parish councils and the like on the same random basis – because modern man needs to be brought into practical contact with administrative and political decisions; people often complain that democracy involves incessant argument and that parliament is a talking shop, but Mill retorts that *of course* democracy is government by discussion, and parliament *ought* to be a talking shop – 600-odd disparate characters cannot govern the country directly, but can discuss the principles on which the government is to be carried on and approve or disapprove the results. In short, the point of democratic institutions is not just to ensure that we are not misgoverned by rascals and jobbing aristocrats but to involve everyone in the process of self-government. The aim is a wide awake, self-governing society, not a prosperous, privatised and thoroughly selfish one.

This has some further implications. If self-government is a good thing, it cannot stop at orthodox politics. Mill extends the argument into the economic realm with gusto. *Pace* some commentators who see Mill as the first Fabian, he was no enthusiast for centralisation and not much concerned with the problem of putting the rational management of the national economy in place of capitalist market-based chaos. The 'anarchy of production' which so distressed Marx and Engels appears to have left him unmoved, even though Marx's best thoughts on the business cycle were simply lifted from Mill. Moreover, he was not a defender of the welfare state – which really is a Fabian invention; he thought that governments ought to provide for the indigent, but he was opposed to any test for eligibility and would have been horrified at the idea of an army of administrators inquiring into clothing needs, cohabitation and the rest. Governments ought to repair income deficiencies and leave everything else to private initiative. But Mill was a sort of socialist all the same; or rather, he was an anti-capitalist, though the word never appears in his pages. What he wanted to replace capitalism was, roughly, workers' co-operatives. State ownership struck him as a long stride towards tyranny; but private property was by no means sacred. One idea was nearly sacred, and that was the idea that as a

man sowed so should he reap – property founded in labour, initiative, intelligence, and so on had a very strong claim on us, but
property founded in nothing better than inheritance, or (like the
property of many landlords) which increased in value fortuitously
or through the efforts of others, had no particular claim. The
question was, what would foster self-government; wage labour is
evidently the antithesis of self-government because the labourer
resigns to the owner all rights of management. This might just about
pass if it were true that the owner bore all the risk of an enterprise
and that all owners took part in active management. But neither
condition was fulfilled. If a firm went bust, the workers suffered
more than the owners; many recipients of profits and capital gains
were mere rentiers, and the mere rentier was entitled to nothing
more than interest payments which would compensate him or her
for deferring their consumption. So, the rights of existing owners
were by no means sacred, and the uninvolvement of workers in
management was a moral scandal. Mill also thought the justice of
the whole system pretty insecure; the defence of capitalism was that
it rewarded effort, but anyone who looked at the labour market
could see that the lowest wages went to those who did the nastiest
jobs. Workers' co-operatives were the way out. In one of his least
successful predictions, Mill gave it as his opinion that within a few
years only the very lowest sort of workman would be willing to work
for an enterprise in whose management he was not associated. As to
how workers' co-operatives should be promoted, Mill argued along
familiar utilitarian lines; that is, governments might foster experi-
ments in co-operation and prevent existing enterprises from ganging
up against them, but there was no question of governments engag-
ing in wholesale expropriation of existing firms for the purpose. It is
not clear whether Mill thought to connect his views on co-operation
with his views on the need for an accessions tax – characteristically,
his aim was to allow us complete freedom to choose to whom we
would leave our wealth, but to prevent anyone from acquiring too
much by merely inheriting it – but it is plausible to think of the two
running in tandem.[13]

This sketch of the way utilitarian ideas were expanded and added
to in order to provide a basis for social democracy is too brief to
carry complete conviction, but I hope it is not too brief to stir some
thoughts about the way in which nineteenth-century ideas can be
drawn on for rather more than the defence of *laissez-faire* conserva-

tism on the one hand or obsolete forms of socialism on the other. My aim has not been to persuade the reader that Mill is admirable because he anticipated many of the ideas of twentieth-century social democrats – Britain might have become a fascist slum in which Mill's works were an underground commodity, and we should think none the worse of him for it; the Tsarist régime which allowed Marx's *Das Kapital* into Russia forbade translations of *On Liberty*. My aim has rather been to suggest that utilitarian ways of thinking which are commonly thought to favour a pretty brutal, pro-capitalist and anti-egalitarian political philosophy may perfectly naturally lead on to something better, and that insofar as Mill's arguments strike a chord, it is because they are impressive, not just because they are familiar.

DISCUSSION ON FOUR

Essentially, Alan Ryan had argued that a commonsense interpretation of utilitarianism, as humanised by J.S. Mill, was a pretty good basis for the conduct of government; there was nothing supernatural or transcendental about it; it fitted the British disposition; it had anti-hierarchical and egalitarian aspects; and Mill's stress on liberty as the capacity for self-government was a direct precursor of SDP thinking.

Some participants accepted that the best public action was likely to be produced on broadly utilitarian lines – and Henry Sidgwick's further refinement of utilitarianism through 'rational benevolence' was cited. It was also supported on the grounds that its rejection of any natural, individual rights and its consequent pooling of utility meant that a collective view was taken of utility; therefore its biggest contribution was that it demanded consensus.

Against utilitarianism it was argued that it was inadequate both as a basis for private morality and as a philosophy of government. If Mill were to be adopted as patron saint, it could not be under the utilitarian banner because Saint Mill was not himself a committed utilitarian. In fact, he was one of the most confused of thinkers. Also, his morally autonomous person – liberated man as a wealth-producing creature – might well become less productive. As argued by Schumpeter, hierarchical structures might well work best for efficiency; utilitarianism had no calculus for resolving this problem.

A further problem, it was suggested, was created by the lack of general acceptance of Mill's vision of individual self-government through a participative democracy; there was plenty of evidence that people on the whole did not have much appetite for the sort of muscular democracy promoted by Mill. After all, most institutions had only a very small number of activists; believers in radical decentralisation with all the decisions pushed down to the lowest possible level had little grounds for encouragement. By the end of the nineteenth century a kind of sociological fatalism had replaced earlier protests against the capitalist divisions of labour; in effect capitalism had constantly bought off claims for greater participation. Finally, middle-class people tended to be strong on theory but dead scared of the initial dislocation inherent in any institutional experiment.

Despite these criticisms Mill's ideas received some support on the grounds that they constituted a considerable advance over Bentham's: liberty was something real for Mill while it was only a residual concept for Bentham. We still had no tradition of rights in Britain; we were stuck with legislative Benthamism. The social democratic approach to rights and the demand for a bill of rights were much more in tune with Mill.

As the discussion developed, we came up against much the same blockage with Mill as with Smith: he was still essentially a pre-industrial thinker. His was still the corn and land model of the economy used by Ricardo. No one until Marx had managed to grasp the idea of a hyper-productive economy and its social implications. It was suggested that Mill, if alive today, would have been panicked by the vested interests in production and would certainly have gone for social audit. Yet though it was possible, with both Smith and Mill, to hazard a guess at how they would have reacted to the modern world, neither Smithian equilibrium nor Millian participation met the challenge posed by the tremendous concentrations of power inherent in large-scale production, which was one of the matters of most concern to modern social democrats. But before leaving the nineteenth century and addressing the problem of excessive private powers it was thought desirable to look at the reservations expressed about the course of the Industrial Revolution by a very different Victorian thinker, John Ruskin, on whom Mark Goyder prepared the following paper.

FIVE

John Ruskin's Victorian Values
The Economic Philosophy of *Unto This Last*

MARK GOYDER

The SDP has suffered in its early years from a shallowness in social criticism. Yes, we are against monetarism, high unemployment, and Thatcherite philistinism on public expenditure. We disavow trade union militancy, unilateralism and state socialism. But against what yardstick do we make these judgements: and what are we for? Half-way along the spectrum between liberty and equality? For an open, classless and more equal society? It sounds clean and rational and modern, but certainly lacks moral substance. Are we anything more than enlightened empiricists, weighing each issue on its merits?

It has been the purpose of our political philosophy study group to suggest that we should be: it is the purpose of this paper to suggest that serious social criticism starts with a clear concept of economic justice – and that nowhere is that expressed so forcefully as in the work of John Ruskin.

John Ruskin was the son of a successful wine merchant, and described himself in the first sentence of his autobiography as 'a violent Tory of the old school'. And yet it was a reading of *Unto This Last* that persuaded Mahatma Gandhi to leave his life as a lawyer in South Africa and go back to fight for justice in India. William Morris, that full-blooded socialist, testifies in an autobiographical aside '. . . how deadly dull the world would have been twenty years ago but for Ruskin. It was through him that I learned to give form to my discontent . . .'[1] And J.A. Hobson, the economist who opened Keynes's eyes to the significance of underconsumption, confesses that Ruskin had a decisive effect upon his entire economic thinking. That is an impressive set of references for an art critic whose first foray into economic criticism was, Kenneth Clark tells us, dismissed at the time as the work of a madman.

After *Unto This Last* Ruskin wrote *Munera Pulveris, Fors Clavigera* and a stream of books and essays which developed his economic thinking. However, as Hobson himself observes with regret, there is no definitive work in which he sets forth his thinking. I have therefore taken as my source the four essays of *Unto This Last*, together with Hobson's own exposition in *John Ruskin – Social Reformer*.

The Roots of Honour

In the first essay, 'The Roots of Honour', Ruskin begins by ridiculing the so-called science of economics with its mistaken belief that:

> The social affections are accidental and disturbing elements in human nature; but avarice and the desire of progress are constant elements. Let us eliminate the inconstants, and considering the human being merely as a covetous machine, examine by what laws of labour, purchase and sale the greatest accumulative result in wealth is attainable.[2]

Now, says Ruskin, all kinds of theories might be constructed from these premises. But they do not seem to explain the world around us: witness, for example, 'the late strikes of our workmen'. You can't, like some theorists, say that workers' and employers' interest are always in conflict; nor can you say that they are one.

> The varieties of circumstances which influence these reciprocal interests are so endless, that all endeavour to deduce rules of action from balance of expediency is vain. No man ever knew, or can know, what will be the ultimate result to himself, or to others, of any given line of conduct. But every man may know, and most of us do know, what is a just and unjust act.[3]

Ruskin goes on to trace the link between this justice and efficiency. It is unselfish treatment of the servant that produces the most effective return for his master. The best officer in the army is the one who inspires the most trust. But then move into manufacturing and we find a paradox – more corporate loyalty is to be found in a gang of thieves than among cotton mill operatives. Why the contrast?

Because, says Ruskin, manufacturing is dominated by the pseudo-scientific view of labour as a factor of production which you hire for as little as you can get away with, and fire as soon as you need it no more. People are victims of the grab-what-we-can mentality that has led to the late strikes of our workmen'. This debased view of human beings does not govern the way soldiers or doctors or pastors work. Why should it govern the way merchants work?

To change attitudes, says Ruskin, we need first to regulate wages for all jobs – just as we already regulate them for the important ones. 'We do not sell our prime ministership by Dutch auction.'[4] Pay the fair wage and sack people if they do a shoddy job: don't let the free workings of the labour market expose you to cheap labour and shoddy results.

The second answer is to tackle a macro-economic problem – the insufficiency of demand. This, says Ruskin, is the great unsolved problem – solve it and there is no obstacle to the just organisation of labour. The trade cycle distorts, demeans, disfigures humanity – has people slaving sixty hours while the demand is there, and then laid off, unwanted, when it slumps.

The Veins of Wealth

It is in the second essay, 'The Veins of Wealth', that Ruskin introduces his crucial distinction between *mercantile* and *political* economy. The conventional view of economics is that it is the science of getting rich – and that a nation full of acquisitive individuals will be a rich nation. But Ruskin points out that rich is a relative term – that the guinea in your pocket is only worth having because someone else needs it. An estate of fruitful land, with gold in its gravel and large herds in its pastures, is little use without people to work it for you, and people will only work it for you if they lack what you have. And so to Ruskin's definition of 'mercantile economy': it signifies ' . . . the accumulation, in the hands of individuals, of legal or moral claim upon, or power over, the labour of others; every such claim implying precisely as much poverty or debt on one side, as it implies riches or right on the others.'[5]

Political economy, on the other hand, ' . . . consists simply in the production, preservation, and distribution, at fittest time and place, of useful and pleasurable things. The farmer who cuts his hay at the right time; the shipwright who drives his bolts home in sound wood; the builder who lays good bricks in well-tempered mortar; the housewife who takes care of her furniture in the parlour and guards against all haste in her kitchen; and the singer who rightly disciplines and never overstrains her voice; are all political economists in the true and final sense adding continually to the riches and wellbeing of the nation to which they belong.'[6]

Mercantile economics is about establishing the maximum

inequality in one's own favour. It *may* add nothing to the wealth of the nation: inequality can be useful or harmful, depending how it is established, and how it is used. For example, if you have two men farming on a desert island and a third plying between them trading in the products that each of the first two can sell to the other, the third man can easily manufacture shortages that quickly make him very rich at the expense of the destitution of his fellow citizens, but in doing so he will improverish the island community as a whole by so weakening the other two.

So the question for the community is not one of individuals getting rich, but of justice in economic behaviour. You cannot look at wealth and tell whether it means good or evil to the community; it depends where it came from and how it is then used. 'One mass of money is the result of action which has created – another of action which has annihilated . . .'[7] A little later Ruskin tells us, 'None of these things you can know. One thing only you can know, namely whether this dealing of yours is a just and faithful one, which is all you need concern yourself about respecting it; sure thus to have done your part in bringing about ultimately in the world a state of things which will not issue in pillage or in death.'[8]

There we have an economic doctrine which does rather more than leave the market to get on with its allocation of resources; which suggests that there is a right and a wrong way to behave in the market place; and that simply leaving all entrepreneurs, property developers, city sharks, and foreign exchange dealers free to maximise their own advantage is both economically and morally wrong.

Ruskin then offers us a prescient footnote. Money is supposed to bring us power over human beings; but there are other ways of motivating people – invisible gold, as Ruskin describes it. What's more, with some of our recent strikes we don't seem to have used this power of money too well to assist our dominance. Perhaps, he muses, we will eventually come to accept that it is the people themselves who are the wealth, and not the money.

The phrase itself, 125 years later, is something of a cliché, the observations all too apt. The power to pay wages conveys less than ever the power to dominate men and women: the need for that invisible gold that wins trust and commitment from employees has never been so pressing. How do we get businesses to satisfy the deep-seated desire for justice in their workforce? That remains invisible

gold for which governments and indeed the whole community must
search.

Qui Judicatis Terram

Diligite justitiam qui judicatis terram means 'love justice, ye who
judge the earth', and in this third essay Ruskin is trying to apply the
principles of justice to the setting of wages. He concludes:

1) That it is possible to work out a just price, or valuation, of
labour as of any other commodity.
2) There is no economic loss by sticking to the just wage: in the
first round of employment, you employ less people at fully just
wages than you would at half wages; but thereafter the properly
paid labour has the spare income to spend which creates
subsidiary employment.

This is one of the least interesting parts of *Unto This Last*. The
world has moved on. Today one can cite cases where it is the trade
union, overriding the employer, which maintains an unjust (because
excessive) wage, with inefficient restrictions on productivity. And
international competition, a factor not mentioned in *Unto This Last*,
makes for circumstances where the payment of an unjust wage
might be the only way to compete with Korea. The application of
political economy to international trade is many times more complex than Ruskin's one-nation model.

However difficult the application of the principle of just payment
within Britain, it does remain a central question for Alliance
politics. There was outrage when judges and civil servants were
awarded a pay increase larger than the annual salary of many
teachers. In our world, the government is such a large employer that
it is shipwrecked unless it can develop some clear principles of just
payment within the public sector and between private and public
sectors.

The third essay also contains another prophetic footnote – this
time on unemployment. Let's be clear, demands Ruskin: do we
regard work as an expensive luxury to be shared amongst us all, or
are we concerned to see that everyone has a source of income? 'Is it
employment that we want to find, or support during unemployment? Is it idleness we wish to put an end to, or hunger? We have to
take up both questions in succession, only not both at the same
time.'[9] Work is a *luxury* we all need to *indulge* in – even the 'idle'
rich, Ruskin concludes. But equally, like all luxuries, it can be over-

indulged. The redistribution of work, and the loosening of the dependence of all citizens upon waged work, are two contemporary problems into which a far-sighted Victorian would appear to have probed a little further than some twentieth-century exponents of Victorian values.

Ad Valorem

And so to 'On Value', the last of the four essays, which starts with a demolition of Mill's definitions of value as exchange value, and Ricardo's definition of value as value for use. Ruskin proposes instead that 'To be "valuable" is to avail towards life.'[10] '. . . the real science of political economy . . . is that which teaches nations to desire and labour for the things that lead to life; and which teaches them to scorn and destroy the things that lead to destruction.'[11]

For a definition of wealth, Ruskin accepts Mill's definition: 'To be wealthy is to have a large stock of useful articles'. But he proceeds to take to pieces the words 'have' and 'useful'. A dead man at the bottom of the ocean with two hundred pounds of gold wrapped round his waist does not 'have' wealth. To have wealth you must be in a position to make use of it. 'Useful' depends on the capacities of the user – wine can do good (says the wine merchant's son) but it can also be destructive. Hence wealth is what we do with it . . . 'The possession of the valuable by the valiant'.[12]

On price, by which Ruskin means exchange value, we are offered the following conclusion: 'There must be advantage on both sides . . . to the persons exchanging; and just payment for his time, intelligence and labour, to any intermediate person effecting the transaction . . . and whatever pay is given to the intermediate person, should be thoroughly known to all concerned.'[13] Ruskin is scornful about the kind of transaction which exploits the ignorance of one party. He draws a withering distinction between 'exchange' and 'acquisition'. If in the exchange one man gains for minimal labour what another man has taken many hours to make, he 'acquires' some of the other man's labour. His gain is the other's loss.

> In mercantile language, the person who thus acquires is said to have 'made a profit' and I believe that many of our merchants are seriously under the impression that it is possible for everybody, somehow, to make a profit in this manner . . . Unhappily for the progress of the science of political economy . . . the pluses make a very positive and venerable appearance in the world . . . whereas

the minuses have, on the other hand, a tendency to retire into back streets, and other places of shade – or even to get themselves wholly and finally put out of sight in graves.[14]

Labour, says Ruskin, is the contest of the life of man with an opposite. There is positive and negative labour – the most positive being the rearing of children, and the most negative that which produces death (note again that Ruskin's definition of work ranges way beyond the work we define as a 'job' – all work, waged or unwaged, is part of his political economy).

Capital is material by which some derivative or secondary good is produced. It is only valuable when, eventually, it results in consumption. There are two kinds of production in an economy – production for the ground and production for the mouth. Production for the ground is only useful with future hope of harvest. Investment is only as valuable as the eventual return in consumption.

> The want of any clear sight of this fact is capital error, issuing in rich interest and revenue of error among the political economists. Their minds are continually set on money gain, not on mouth gain . . . they are like children trying to jump on the heads of their own shadows; the money gain being only the shadow of the true gain, which is humanity. The final object of political economy, therefore, is to get good method of consumption, and great quantity of consumption: in other words, to use everything and use it nobly.[15]

Perhaps Ruskin's most resounding phrase is, 'There is no wealth but life.'[16]

THE RELEVANCE OF RUSKIN

There will be many technocratic social democrats who think we have little to learn from a nineteenth-century economic moralist like Ruskin.

The SDP's Political Economy

For as long as Tories stay Thatcherite, and socialists stay syndicalist, it is easy for the SDP to prosper under the banner of moderate modernity. But the time is coming when Tories and Labour alike will converge on to the middle ground, each with their familiar battle-cries – the Conservatives as the one-nation party, and Labour as the party of industrial revival, the pensioner and the health service patient. Moderation is no banner for these times. A commitment to the social market is a little more distinctive, but has the disadvantage of being incomprehensible to the voter. We have to communicate a distinctive philosphy, and one to which voters can instinctively respond.

The appeal to economic justice is the natural banner of the Alliance parties. With Ruskin we can condemn the Thatcherite economy as a denial of economic justice. Mrs Thatcher represents the victory of mercantile, grab-what-you-can-while-you-can economics: she believes that a nation of get-rich-quick shopkeepers will be a wealthy nation. We believe that there is no wealth but life; and our political economy demands that we mobilise the contribution of *all* our citizens. Mercantile economics allows you to claim success in the south while the north decays, or in the suburbs while cities rot, or to boast of rising output when 13% of the workforce lies idle. Political economics has a different aim – to use everything, and to use it nobly. In Ruskin's humane version of economics it is as important to ensure a good quality of life and contribution from all citizens, as to ensure the maximum quantity of output.

In Ruskin's political economy the contributions made by carers, parents, young volunteers, public servants, artists, amateur gardeners, are as important as those of the electronics industry. Ruskin would not be impressed by the Lord Young view of economic usefulness which has every fourteen-year-old at the controls of a computer – not because it is useless to have people numerate but because it is narrow to be obsessed by it. Production for the ground is ultimately only as important as the consumption it eventually makes possible. It is valid to ask where the money is coming from – but equally valid to ask to what ultimate living purpose we are producing whatever it is we produce.

Quality of Output

It might be acceptable to Mrs Thatcher to have a rising national income built on the production of nuclear weapons and the proliferation of amusement arcades but that does not represent an increase in wealth in Ruskin's terms, or ours. The distinction between mercantile and political economy is also the distinction between the kind of ruthless expansionism that cares not for concrete ugliness, or hedgerows laid waste, or the green growth which the SDP has – albeit belatedly – espoused. 'The final outcome and consummation of all wealth is in the producing, as many as possible, full-breathed, bright-eyed and happy-hearted human beings.'[17]

Work, Life and Income

Political economics, insists Ruskin, includes all creative activity – craftmanship, child-rearing, continuing education, as well as straight commerce. The purpose of economic activity is to enable all these things to be done. It is *not* simply to create as many full-time tedious jobs as possible. This means a thorough rethink of the relationship between life, work and income. Currently, life without a job means life as an outcast. The Ruskin version would allow life without a traditional, waged job, certainly without a full-time job. It would allow financial support to the single parent bringing up children, to the person who wanted to combine part-time paid employment with voluntary work or increased leisure. It would penalise, though not necessarily prohibit, the obsessive sixty-hour-a-week work patterns all too often found in the salaried and wage-earning sector, and promote a fairer distribution of available waged work along with a social dividend and greater social acceptability for unwaged work.

Political economy means mobilising from the community the maximum human contribution; revolutionising work patterns, and loosening the connections between work and income-support. That is a much more complicated and thorough change than that suggested by the phrase 'social market'. Where the social market implies separate compartments (the 'competitive' economy and the 'compassionate' community; the 'tough' market section and the 'tender' services), political economy suggests an interweaving of fair treatment and efficient operation within the market sector, and the same insistence, in market and non-market sectors alike, upon the job well but not ruthlessly done, for its own and the consumer's sake rather than for acquisitive reasons.

Economic Organisation and Economic Justice

Economic justice is the key to efficiency. A nation in which large sections are unjustly excluded from the rewards for economic success will be an unproductive nation – hence the importance of rethinking the relationship between life, work and income.

The principle of economic justice – or fairness – remains also a much better principle for governing the workings of a company or industry than the overworked concept of industrial democracy, advocated in the 1960s and 70s by those who stopped short of workers' control.

Industrial democracy does not tell you how a government should deal with a group like the miners whose whole way of life becomes threatened by the declining competitiveness of their product. Whether or not you involve a threatened workforce in harsh decisions, you do not escape the problem. You can, however, measure the response of a government or a workforce by the yard-stick of fairness. That implies weighing the conflicting claims of tax-payer, employer, employee and consumer. It implies that you neither throw unwanted people or communities suddenly on the scrapheap, nor do you allow them to claim forever the right to employment in a dying industry; that you consider the alternative possibilities for investment, and weigh the obligations of protecting people from shock against wider costs to the taxpayer and other claims upon his money.

Of course economic justice does not exclude industrial demo-cracy: it simply has a wider application. Fairness within the enter-prise means giving to employees, as to shareholders, what is their due, and this must include rewarding a sustained investment of effort with an assured share of the profit; it must imply some eclipse in the absolute power of the shareholders to buy and sell the company over the heads of a long-established workforce; if there is no wealth but life, then you cannot accept that companies change hands overnight, or over anguished months of boardroom manoeuvring, without reference to the wishes of their employees. A constitutional means has to be found to redress the balance.

In 'Qui Judicatis Terram' Ruskin asked, what are the laws of jus-tice concerning the payment of labour. We have to devise methods of payment within the enterprise which tend towards co-operation, which assert the role of employees as partners with a share in the future profits rather than as wage slaves with only self- or 'mercan-tile' interest in short-term grab-what-you-can. And in the public sector, we have to devise the means of pay determination that satisfy employees' sense of fairness and render unnecessary the resort to crude methods such as withdrawal of labour.

In an age of advancing specialisation employment becomes more exclusive. The two nations of tomorrow may be, on the one side, the technically sophisticated and on the other, the unskilled and unem-

ployed for whom society offers little dignity or security. Economic
fairness means that the economy's outsiders too must have a share
in its success. 'To use all wealth, and use it nobly', means ensuring
that all citizens, irrespective of ability level, or colour or geography,
are drawn into contributing, even if that contribution is not always
rewarded by a wage packet.

Ruskin and the Decline of the Industrial Spirit?

Martin Wiener, in his important book *English Culture and the
Decline of the Industrial Spirit* (Pelican 1985), identifies Ruskin
along with Arnold, Mill and Dickens as a social critic who turned
attitudes against the new commercialism of the nineteenth century.
But he exaggerates when he says that Ruskin 'is best known for
bringing competition into disrepute. He also, though it has been less
noticed, deprived production of its intrinsic moral value.'[18]

This misrepresents Ruskin's message by ignoring its context.
Ruskin tells us that unregulated competition can throw lives on to a
scrapheap; that a thirst for output, irrespective of the quality of that
output, can scar landscape and way of life. To say these things, in a
time of brash industrial growth, is not to denigrate profit or competition as such. Ruskin was concerned with the framework of justice
within which these mechanisms should operate.

Ruskin was not out to discredit production. He was anxious to
establish the difference between labour and other factors of production. In *The Roots of Honour* he is emphatic that the management of
people in industry matters as much as in any of the more tradition-
ally respectable professions, and he explicitly states that the public
are wrong to despise commerce and goes on: 'They will find that
commerce is an occupation which gentlemen will every day see more
need to engage in . . .'[19]

In fact, Ruskin's heroic definition of the leadership task of the
good merchant would strike chords with one of America's current
entrepreneurs, Ross Perot, who said recently: 'We need to strike out
the word management. You will never get anything done through
management. You need to get it done with leadership.'[20]

There are many occasions when Ruskin goes too far – he condemns all interest as usury, Hobson tells us;[21] and elsewhere in *Unto
This Last* he says that government and co-operation are in all things
the law of life, and anarchy and competition in all things the law of
death. Experience since 1860 suggests that government is not always

synonymous with co-operation, nor competition with anarchy! It is fruitless to apply directly Ruskin's Victorian solutions or indeed to follow all his judgements. What we can do is to take from Ruskin those three key insights – into the wholeness and dependence upon living people of the economic system which he calls political economy; into the concept of economic justice as the governing principle for all our trading and institution-building; and into the loosening of the boundaries that we need between employment, living, and income-support. Out of these insights we can fashion an economic doctrine which pursues efficiency based on fair foundations, which can appeal to the common man's instinct for fairness.

We can audit the nation's performance against the yardstick of how many full-breathed, bright-eyed and happy-hearted human beings it is likely to produce, and we can preserve a distinctive morality of economics, a morality which the SDP and the Alliance need to underpin the public investment and the inflation tax and the expenditure tax and the employee share ownership, and all the other worthwhile technical proposals we have to offer.

The SDP – not just the party of the social market, but the party of economic justice. The fairness party; believing that there is no wealth but life, and reminding the electorate of government's obligation to use all human contribution and to use it nobly.

DISCUSSION ON FIVE

In discussion, Mark Goyder received some criticism for wanting to tear up most subsequent economic history and revert to
the mediaeval concept of the just wage. He countered that
even if you rejected a set minimum wage, you could still move
towards the Meade/Dore idea of a citizens' dividend; there
was already a huge interaction between wages and other
sources of income such as benefits and pensions. We should
therefore be exploring ways into a less wage-based society.

Several participants expressed varying degrees of unhappi-
ness with the slogan phrase 'economic justice', which had the
connotation of equal incomes and did not convey the broader
type of fairness. It was suggested that Ruskin used 'economy'
in a very wide sense; 'economic justice' could only make sense
on a very broad interpretation. Expanding it to 'economic and
financial justice' was then proposed; this would cover interest
rates too. Another colleague had no quarrel with the phrase as
it stood: it was exactly what was needed in a country polarised
between rich and poor, north and south . . . but the concept of
a just wage was indeed mediaeval; if governments wanted
good top management they would have to pay for it. This
point was accepted by Mark Goyder but governments in his
view couldn't leave the market to decide things like teachers'
wages; here fairness did come in; managers added value to
themselves by successful management; teachers didn't; they
only advanced within a very narrow wage band. It was generally agreed that certain 'customary' wages were too rigid and
sticky.

Whilst on wage fixing, a voice was raised on behalf of
consumers: weren't we leaving them out? How did one adjudi-
cate the consumer's claims if wages were fixed (as had been
suggested) on a devolved basis within the context of the firm?
It was notorious that consumers were more difficult to
organise than producers; their organisations were weaker;
government might be seen as their natural protector, yet
governments were always subject to stronger and better
organised producer pressures. It was suggested here that
consumers should be represented on the boards of all public
companies, not just those in the state sector; public limited
companies should be obliged to include a statement of intent

in their articles; one of the roles of democracy was to encourage the creation of responsible institutions. Mergers and takeovers then came under attack; there were frequent job losses and pension rights were often not protected.

Reverting to Ruskin's distinction between mercantile and political economy, concern was expressed that Ruskin was pursuing community rather than market ends but we certainly didn't want a directed or command economy. Mark Goyder acknowledged that Ruskin had gone rather off the rails in holding that competition was anarchy, but insisted that we had to mobilise the contribution of everyone; inputs were extremely uneven at present with many people not allowed to make any input at all and condemned to a passive, impoverished and frustrating existence. It was an important insight of Ruskin's that you could only measure wealth by what it contributed to the quality of life; your activity might not be waged but it was nonetheless part of the economy and wealth of the nation. The importance of political economy as opposed to mere mercantile economy was that it meant an economy for all, including the small entrepreneurs who were crippled by high interest rates. Keynes would have agreed with that – and euthanised the rentiers to boot. Hobson, it was suggested here, made an interesting link between Ruskin and Keynes. At this point Robert Skidelsky gave his opinion that Keynes was not really much influenced by Hobson – though he did pay him a late tribute. Accordingly, Robert Skidelsky was called upon to present a paper on Keynes.

SIX

Keynes's Political Legacy

ROBERT SKIDELSKY

(1) Introduction

John Maynard Keynes often described himself as a man of the Left. In 1926 he wrote 'the republic of my imagination lies on the extreme left of celestial space'.[1] The question, he told Kingsley Martin in 1939, was 'whether we are prepared to move out of the nineteenth-century *laissez-faire* state into that of liberal socialism . . .'[2] The problem with such self-perception is that Keynes rarely championed causes which were distinctively left-wing. Social democracy, then as now, was distinctively about equality. It aimed to bring about a more equal distribution of property, income, rights, life-chances, circumstances. Redistributionary finance received powerful support from the Cambridge school of welfare economics. Keynes was almost completely silent on such issues. There are very few references to equality or social justice in his economic and political writings, and when they occur they do so in much more limited contexts than characterised even moderate socialist usage. What is missing from these writings, therefore, is that which is distinctively *ethical**.

One may speculate on the reasons for this. Economics, like everything else, is subject to a division of labour. At Cambridge Keynes taught the theory of money; the theory of value and distribution was in the hands of Pigou. At one point Keynes invoked a political division of labour as well. Questions of social justice, he said, were best left to the 'party of the proletariat'; Liberals like himself should concern themselves with issues of 'economic efficiency' and 'individual liberty'.[3] Again, Keynes sometimes talked of socialism being

---

* Keynes does talk from time to time about 'arbitrary and inequitable' distribution (see esp. *The General Theory*, 1973, ed.p.372); but he characteristically uses phrases like this when discussing the effects of an unstable value of money (e.g., *Collected Writings*, xix, 160). There is nothing I have found in his work to suggest that he held the long-run distribution of wealth and income ground out by capitalist society to be unjust. Keynes's use of social and political language always needs to be subjected to the closest textual, and contextual, scrutiny.

for 'later', after the economic problem had been solved.[4] That is, he did not regard the question of the distribution of given resources to be as urgent as that of how to obtain full utilisation of potential resources.

I doubt whether such reasons go to the heart of the matter. As Elizabeth Durbin has rightly pointed out, 'the focus on particular problems, the choice between different economic means, and even the use of the economic model rather than another, may . . . be affected by the values of the policy adviser'.[5] Keynes's values were, in important respects, different from those of most socialists. Equality was never a passion for him; indeed Keynes's passions were not importantly political at all.

Any investigation of Keynes's political legacy has to start, then, from his philosophy of life. The most important point to be made here is that Keynes was the child of the Cambridge revolt against Benthamite utilitarianism, the main *secular* philosophical system of Victorian Britain. Bentham sought to direct private and public conduct to the achievement of a single moral end: 'the greatest happiness of the greatest number'; this end being held to be rationally deduced from a factual premise about individuals; namely, that they sought pleasure and tried to avoid pain. The difficulties with Benthamism accumulated during the nineteenth century, and culminated in a frontal attack by G.E. Moore in his *Principia Ethica* (1902) – the most important philosophical influence on Keynes's life. In essence, Moore denied that goodness and happiness are the same thing; that what people *wanted* (happiness or pleasure) is necessarily good for them. Benthamism ceased to be serviceable as a moral philosophy, without necessarily ceasing to serve as a rational basis for politics and economics. This conclusion was fundamental to Keynes; his political legacy cannot be understood apart from it. He never regarded public life as an important arena for the achievement of ethical ends; this severely limited the ethical passion he invested in his politics and economics. Bertrand Russell put the matter with the utmost precision when he wrote of Keynes that 'when he concerned himself with politics and economics he left his soul at home'.[6]

Keynes had problems with another aspect of utilitarianism, its consequentialism. Actions can be justified only by results, i.e. by whether they increase the sum of goodness. But how can we ever have enough advance knowledge of results to be able to say that this or that action is even probably right? Keynes's study of the connection between 'ought' and 'probable' culminated in his *Treatise on Probability*, published in 1921. His epistemology in turn suggested conclusions as to what constituted rational behaviour in politics and economics. His lifelong bias against *long-run thinking* can perhaps be traced to these epistemological investigations.

To the student of politics and economics Keynes's legacy lies in the mixture of scepticism and optimism, timidity and robustness which he brought to the public questions of his day. His was the temper of the 'middle way'.

(2) Politics: Ends and Means

The nearest Keynes got to expounding a theory of politics was in an undergraduate essay on Edmund Burke, which he successfully submitted for the University Members' Prize for English Essay in the summer of 1904.[7] Keynes showed himself to be largely sympathetic to the views of the founder of British Conservatism. He approved of Burke's separation of ethics and politics, also his preference for present over future goods. He criticised him for excessive timidity as a reformer, and for undervaluing the claims of truth; in general for carrying reasonable propositions too far.

Burke's 'unparalleled political wisdom', according to Keynes, lay in the fact that he was the first thinker consistently to base a theory of politics on utilitarianism rather than on abstract rights, though it was a utilitarianism 'modified' by the principle of equity – governments should avoid artificial discrimination against individuals or classes. He quotes him approvingly: 'The question with me is, not whether you have a right to render your people miserable, but whether it is not in your interest to make them happy'. Keynes adds: 'This is not a very recondite doctrine, but to Burke must be given the credit of first clearly and insistently enunciating it'. Today this interpretation of Burke would be considered mistaken. Modern commentators say that Burke believed in natural law, the organic state and the religious foundation of politics. But it is what Keynes believed Burke to believe that is important for our purposes.

An important conclusion follows. If the government's business is want-satisfaction, it follows that promotion of economic prosperity is a proper concern of statesmanship. Moreover, a government which promotes welfare in this sense will run little risk of diminishing goodness, for up to a point the requirements of both coincide.

Keynes also endorses another key principle of Burke's: that the happiness or utility which governments should aim to maximise is *short-run* not *long-run*. The following portmanteau quotation gives the gist of Keynes's argument:

> Burke ever held, and held rightly, that it can seldom be right . . . to sacrifice a present benefit for a doubtful advantage in the future . . . It is not wise to look too far ahead; our powers of prediction are slight, our command over remote results infinitesimal. It is therefore the happiness of our own contemporaries that is our main concern; we should be very chary of sacrificing large numbers of people for the sake of a contingent end, however advantageous that end may appear . . . We can never know enough to make the chance worth taking . . . There is this further consideration that is often in need of emphasis: it is not sufficient that the state of affairs which we seek to promote should be better than the state of affairs which preceded it; it must be sufficiently better to make up for the evils of the transition.[8]

Keynes's handling of Burke's views on property and democracy in the light of such 'maxims' of statesmanship is worth particular notice. Burke defended existing property rights on the double ground that redistribution of wealth would make no real difference to the poor, since the poor greatly outnumbered the rich, while at the same time it would 'considerably reduce in numbers those who could enjoy the undoubted benefits of wealth and who could confer on the state the advantages which the presence of wealthy citizens always brings'. Keynes felt this argument 'undoubtedly carries very great weight; in certain conceivable types of communities it is overwhelming; and it must always be one of the most powerful rejoinders to any scheme which has equalisation as its ultimate aim.' But its validity is 'very much less' if directed against (i) 'any attempt to influence the channels in which wealth flows', and (ii) the relief of starvation or acute poverty. Burke's method was not valid, Keynes wrote, against estate duties 'whose object is to mulct great masses of accumulation', nor against the expropriation of feudal estates during the French Revolution.[9] The argument is that where there is great degradation, and subsequent discontent, the balance of expediency shifts towards redistribution: Burke is often so concerned to defend the 'outworks' that he does not see that this might endanger the 'central system' itself.[10]

Keynes never believed that the maintenance of the 'central

system' of Britain in his day required large-scale confiscation of property. In *The Economic Consequences of the Peace* he wrote of pre-war Britain that 'The greater part of the population, it is true, worked hard and lived at a low standard of comfort, yet were, to all appearances, reasonably contented with this lot. But escape was possible, for any man of capacity or character at all exceeding the average, into the middle and upper classes . . .'[11] At the same time, he insisted that governments must have discretion to revise contracts between the living and the dead, since 'the powers of uninterrupted usury are too great'. It was the 'absolutists of contract' he wrote in his *Tract on Monetary Reform* (1923) 'who are the parents of Revolution' – a good Burkean attitude, though one that Burke sometimes ignored.[12]

The issue of democracy, Keynes insisted, involved two separate questions. Has the mass of people a right to direct self-government? Is it expedient and conducive to good government that there should be more self-government? To both questions Burke returned an 'uncompromising negative'. On the first, Keynes stood solidly with Burke. Government is simply a 'contrivance of human wisdom' to 'supply certain . . . wants; and that is the end of the matter'. People, that is, are entitled to good government, not self-government. The more difficult question is whether self-government is a necessary means to good government, and here Keynes is more open than Burke. He agrees with him that 'the people' are incompetent to govern themselves, and that parliament must always be prepared to resist popular prejudice in the name of equity between individuals and classes. But he criticises Burke's 'dream of a representative class', which underpinned his defence of rotten boroughs and restricted franchise, on the ground that no one class can adequately represent the feelings or interests of the whole. Burke also underestimated the educative value of self-government.

Nevertheless, Keynes doubted whether any 'rational or unprejudiced body of men' would have ever dared to make the experiment in universal suffrage had they not been 'under the influence of a fallacious notion concerning natural political rights'. But whatever the ultimate fate of this experiment, so far democracy had not disgraced itself. This was because its 'full force had not yet come into operation'. First, 'whatever be the numerical representation of wealth, its power will always be out of all proportion.' Secondly, 'the defective organisation of the newly enfranchised classes has prevented any revolutionary alteration in the pre-existing balance of power.'[13]

Running through Keynes's commentary is a utilitarian attitude to rights. If people are made discontented by the absence of 'rights', then rights should be conceded – but as a means to good government. It was the typical Whig attitude to reform.

Keynes's criticisms of Burke issued on three main points: 'his preference for peace over truth, his extreme timidity in introducing present evil for the sake of future benefits, and his disbelief in men's acting rightly, except on the rarest occasions, because they have judged that it is right to act.' As Keynes notes, these contentions are all related to Burke's central epistemological position, that we can never be certain enough of the truth to choose rationally between different courses of action. This being so it is better to fall back on tradition.[14] In other words, Burke denied the value of the pursuit of truth on the ground that it would disturb the peace of the Commonwealth (a present good) without giving any assurance of a greater benefit in the future.

This was a conclusion which Keynes wanted to resist. As he put it: 'It is usually admitted that, whatever the immediate consequences of a new truth may be, there is a high probability that truth will in the long run lead to better results than falsehood.'

He conceded, however, that 'the modern prejudice in favour of truth [may be] founded on somewhat insufficient bases.'[15] He had nothing more to add to this in his essay on Burke. But he had already started to develop a theory of probability explicitly designed to improve the epistemological foundations of rational choice; it is to this that we now turn.

The influence of Keynes's theory of probability on his economics is at last starting to be discussed;[16] but there has been no attempt to relate it to his theory of politics. The problem with which Keynes grappled is inherent in any consequentialist theory. If the rightness of actions is to be judged by their effects, action must be informed by a knowledge of probable consequences. This immediately raises the question of our power to predict future events. Statistical or empirical probability is part of our predictive system. It tells us that an event A will occur in a certain ratio to event B. The basis for such predictions lies in the high degree of regularity exhibited by certain natural and artificial arrangements. The existence of statistical probability is what makes possible insurance against risk. But the theory is much less relevant when applied to most *social* arrangements where, as Keynes remarked, our power of predicting all but the most immediate consequence of our actions rapidly dwindles to zero, either because there are no statistical probabilities or because we lack knowledge of them. The conclusion Moore drew from this is that we ought to obey the law and follow the 'rules' of correct behaviour; since the adverse consequences of disregarding them, from the individual point of view, are likely to be high, while the benefits are indeterminate. Moore's consequentialism led him towards conservative morality; Burke's towards conservative politics.

Keynes wanted to escape from a train of argument which put an excessive premium on tradition. The only way he saw of doing so was to disconnect the notion of probability from that of prediction. He did this by developing his *logical* theory of probability. There could be probabilities, Keynes argued, without frequencies, or knowledge of frequencies. The probable is not what is likely to happen, but what it is rational to believe will happen given our information; it has to do with the bearing of evidence on conclusions; we can say that our actions are probably right independently of whether our expectations are realised or disappointed. Probability is thus not a prediction ('This will happen more or less often if that happens') but a logical judgement about the relationship between the premise (evidence) and conclusion of an argument ('It is reasonable to believe *that* conclusion to *this* extent'). This formulation opened up a wide field to *rational* discretionary action which both Moore and Burke seemed to have closed off. To make an estimate of a probability was simply to think rationally about consequences when there were no frequencies. Rational judgement was not so easily defeated as Moore (or for that matter Burke) believed.

The policy conclusion which Keynes attributed to Burke – that 'it is the happiness of our own contemporaries which should concern us' – is not thereby upset, since Keynes's probabilities are based on circumstances which change by the very fact of us acting on them. But Keynes believed that he had developed a more rational theory of means, one that allowed greater scope for reason, judgement, and discretion than Burke was willing to concede. If Burke was sceptical about reform, Keynes was sceptical about tradition. He took the distinctively Enlightenment position that tradition was a repository of falsehood, which could be dissipated by allowing reason to play on the facts. His theory of probability was thus designed to strengthen the claims of reason against those of tradition.* For these reasons Keynes cannot be classified as a Burkean Conservative, much as he sympathised with Burke's general position. His 'prejudice' in favour of truth was too great. This was to dominate the work of his maturity.

(3) The Reconstruction of Liberalism
Keynes was a lifelong liberal – with a small and large 'l'. By the inter-war years the tasks of liberal statesmanship had emerged with painful clarity: to stave off revolution from left and right and to make the economic system (or 'capitalism') work more efficiently and humanely. The two tasks were connected, the second being a means to the first: for by the 1930s both communism and fascism were staking their claim to power on liberal capitalism's inability to provide full employment. This premise Keynes set out to refute. 'The authoritarian state systems of to-day' he wrote in *The General Theory* 'seem to solve the problem of unemployment at the expense of efficiency and freedom. It is certain that the world will not much longer tolerate the unemployment which . . . is associated – and, in my opinion, inevitably associated – with present day capitalistic individualism. But it may be possible by a right analysis of the problem to cure the disease whilst preserving efficiency and freedom.'[17]

Taking a broad historical view, the Keynesian revolution in economics was a key part of what emerged as the dominant Western intellectual response to the rise of the totalitarians and, more generally, to the 'rise of the masses'. Keynes's reconstruction of economics, Schumpeter's reformulation of democratic theory, Mannheim's programme for the social sciences, Popper's work on the logic of scientific discovery can all be seen as part of the intellectual re-equipment of liberalism to meet the threats to it. Keynes's achievement is the more impressive as being, uniquely, that of a non-emigré – someone who had not suffered personally from the

* Whether it succeeded is open to question. The trouble with his theory of probability is that knowledge of probabilities (in his sense) is a matter of logical intuition. This exposed him to Ramsey's famous retort: '[Keynes] supposes that, at any rate in certain cases, [probability relations] can be perceived; but speaking for myself I feel confident that this is not true. I do not perceive them . . .' (F.P. Ramsey, *The Foundations of Mathematics and Other Logical Essays*, ed. R.B. Braithwaite, [1931], p.161.)

breakdown of the liberal order.

This intellectual movement may be called the second liberal revival. Unlike the 'new' liberalism of the turn of the century, it made no serious attempt to reshape the philosophical foundations of liberalism. 'New' liberals like Leonard Hobhouse were concerned chiefly with the justifications of existing property relations, from the point of view of efficiency and equity, and as affecting the moral growth of the individual. By contrast the second wave of liberal thinkers took the existing property relationships as given: what they did was to superimpose a managerial philosophy on the theory and practice of 'classic' liberalism. This reflects, on the one hand, a much greater institutional timidity, in face of the violent rearrangement of property relations which had taken place in Russia; on the other, a faith that existing institutions could be made to work provided that government intervened in certain key areas and that the social sciences could provide an ideologically neutral logic of intervention – a faith which may have been born of desperation. A philosophy of *ad hoc* intervention based on disinterested thought was thus twentieth-century liberalism's answer to the faith of early nineteenth-century liberals that institutional reform could secure the conditions of minimalist government – a belief, of course, which Marx also shared. It reflects the extent to which utilitarianism had lost its radical cutting edge.*

In Keynes's updated version of liberalism the intellectual has a key part to play in stabilising society – as social scientist and as manager. Keynes believed that the economic problem of his day was an intellectual and not a structural or institutional problem: the slump was the result of a 'frightful muddle',[18] whose cure lay, first in the realm of thought, and secondly in that of management.

---

* This interpretation of Keynes's work was first suggested to me by Maurice Cranston who wrote:
  If we consider the line of British liberal theorising that goes from J.S. Mill through T.H. Green to L.T. Hobhouse, we can see how the central idea of liberty is first transposed from the idea of individual freedom into one of social freedom, and then transformed from social freedom into social justice . . . we find liberalism . . . to be mainly a doctrine of social and economic betterment and hardly at all a doctrine of individual rights . . . But Keynes stands apart from this endeavour to modernise liberalism by transforming its philosophy. What he tried deliberately, if somewhat deviously, to do, was to preserve the essential core of classical liberalism by attaching to it certain practical policies which he chose to

Keynes has often been criticised for exaggerating the importance of ideas relative to power, especially class power. According to the Marxist John Strachey, his *Essays in Persuasion* were so 'uniformly unpersuasive' because he ignored the fact that unemployment was a necessary feature of capitalism.[19] Keynes compounded his political naivety, from this point of view, by writing in *The General Theory*: 'But soon or late, it is ideas, not vested interests, which are dangerous for good or evil.'[20]

It is a facile misinterpretation of Keynes's position to say that he believed that ideas triumph by a kind of natural magic. Successful ideas succeed because they have more political utility than the alternatives on offer; smaller interests yield to larger interests, or survive only if they can plausibly attach themselves to coalitions of interests. Here public opinion, as filtered through the electoral process, is ultimately decisive in a democracy. Far from believing in the unsupported power of ideas, Keynes wrote in 1922: 'Even if economists and technicians knew the secret remedy, they could not apply it until they had persuaded the politicians; and the politicians, who have ears but no eyes, will not attend to the persuasion until it reverberates back to them as an echo from the great public.'[21] Politicians, being in the business of want-satisfaction, have to attend to public opinion sooner or later, if they are to win or retain power; and public opinion will not stand indefinitely for policies which they perceive as bringing about impoverishment. Having said this, it is also true that Keynes was the last person to deny the power of persuasive utterance. He was himself a master of it, and it was through his journalism that the educated public, at any rate, became familiar with his general approach to curing the slump.

call socialistic. Yet in doing this, Keynes seems to me to go straight back to the simple liberalism of Locke, and not in any way to subscribe to the idealistic and metaphysical philosophy of radical liberalism which emerged after J.S. Mill . . . The sort of 'state control' Keynes envisaged was always organisational and not confiscatorial. (Maurice Cranston, 'Keynes's Political Ideas and Their Influence', in A.P. Thirwall (ed.) *Keynes and Laissez-Faire*, (1978), pp.110–2).

For a different view, see Peter Clarke 'The Politics of Keynesian Economics, 1924–1931', in Michael Bentley and John Stevenson (eds.), *High and Low Politics in Modern Britain*, (1983), pp.155–81. Clarke writes (p.175), '. . . Keynes's political outlook . . . remained in essentials that of new Liberalism which had flourished in the Edwardian period when he was a young man.'

With intellectuals (and in this case economists) the process of acceptance of new ideas is admittedly more complicated. Economists too have political purposes, and are open to non-rational 'persuasion'. But genuine intellectual conversion also has to take place. Theories must possess formal properties of logical consistency which commend them to specialists. However, it would be wrong to say that Keynes attached excessive importance to this factor. What he tended to require of fellow-economists was the power of 'seeing the world' as he saw it; minds must meet intuitively before logical discussion could become fruitful. But such 'meeting of minds' was never for him simply or largely a matter of psychological affinity. His faith was that all rational (and competent) persons confronted with the same evidence will attach the same values to various possible conclusions to be drawn from it.

For Keynes, therefore, the success or failure, as well as the truth or falsity, of ideas was always connected to the facts. Those ideas win which have a perceived tendency to maximise contentment; for intellectuals the probable rightness of a theory is a matter of logical intuition applied to the evidence. These are straightforward deductions from his political utilitarianism and from his theory of probability. It is significant that Marxists, who started in the 1930s by saying that Keynes's ideas could not possibly be implemented under capitalism, ended up by explaining that they 'fitted the needs' of capitalism. Keynes could not, I think, have asked for more.

Keynes has also been criticised for his belief in the possibility of disinterested economic management. Seymour Harris accused him of failing to 'reconcile his dislike and distrust of politicians with his determination to thrust upon government serious additional responsibilities.'[22] Alternatively, he has been attacked for believing that economic management could be 'insulated' from political pressures.

In considering such criticisms it is important to be clear about what Keynes wanted his 'managers' to do. Keynes's (not Keynesian) policies for securing a high, continuous, non-inflationary level of output and employment can be divided into two main parts: 'a somewhat comprehensive socialisation of investment';[23] and monetary fine-tuning.[24] Fiscal fine-tuning was not part of his design; budget deficits were to be resorted to only to pull an economy out of a slump. The post-war reliance on managing the economy through budgetary policy, with monetary policy either ignored or reduced to a subsidiary role, was not part of Keynes's original intention. The short answer to Seymour Harris, therefore, is that Keynes did *not* wish to thrust large extra responsibilities on politicians as such. He can still be held to be politically naive in supposing that they could be prevented from using the potential instruments for manipulating demand to their own political advantage.

In trying to understand how Keynes visualised the political economy of the future, a key problem of interpretation is posed by the phrase 'a somewhat comprehensive socialisation of investment'. It is clear enough that Keynes means that *the state* will become responsible for a major part of total investment. Thus he writes in the *General Theory*, 'I expect to see the State, which is in a position to calculate the marginal efficiency of capital-goods on long views and on the basis of the general social advantage, taking an ever greater responsibility for directly organising investments . . .'[25] The problem here is to determine what Keynes means by 'the State'. It is highly improbable that Keynes wants to identify the state with the government of the day; since he can hardly have supposed that politicians elected to govern on the basis of renewable popular consent would be best placed to take 'long views'. At the very least we must suppose Keynes to mean the permanent officials; but by the state he seems to mean something wider still. Take, for example, the following letter he wrote to *The Times* on 25 March 1925 (my italics added):

So far from wishing to diminish the authority of the Bank of England I regard that great institution as a heaven-sent gift, ideally suited to be the instrument of the reforms I advocate. We have here a semi-independent corporation *within the State*, with immense prestige and historical tradition, not in fact working for private profit, with no interest whatever except the public good, yet detached from the wayward influence of politics . . . The Bank of England is a type of that *socialism* of the future which is in accord with the British instincts of government, and which – perhaps one may hope – our Commonwealth is evolving within its womb. The Universities are another example of the semi-independent institutions divested of private interest which I have in mind. *The State* is generally sterile and creates little. New forms and modes spring from the fruitful minds of individuals. But when a corporation, devised by private resource, has reached a certain age and a certain size, it *socialises* itself, or falls into decay. But none perhaps, except the Bank of England – and (should I add?) *The Times* newspaper – has yet completed the process. I differ from the immediate policy of the Bank of England; but it is on the greatness and prestige of this institution . . . that I rest my hopes for the future.[26]

The clarity of language in this letter is not ideal; but the gist of what Keynes is saying is both understandable and interesting. He means by the state that sector of the polity not working for private self-interest but for the public good. This cuts across the division between the public and private sectors; the state includes bodies which are legally private, but which in the course of their evolution have come to acquire a sense of public purpose. Insofar as politicians were motivated by public purposes they were part of the state; insofar as they pursued their own interests through politics they were part of the non-state. Governments were presumably a mixture of both.

All this may sound very strange, but Keynes's language has its roots in the past, when the sovereign, or prince, was *both* ruler *and* private landlord, with public and private interests inextricably intertwined. The difficulty Keynes found in expressing his thoughts in clear language also testifies to the lack in Britain of any adequate modern theory of the state. In constitutional law the state in Britain is the Crown-in-Parliament and its servants; but in mediaeval times sovereignty was fragmented through the system of vassalage by which grants of land were invested with juridical and political powers. In the capitalist era property escaped from vassalage to become fully 'privatised'; with its public functions taken over by the Crown-in-Parliament. In effect, Keynes suggested that this tendency was now reversing itself. The state was no longer rigidly separated from private property and private enterprise: rather the two were forging or re-forging a corporate relationship. 'Time and the Joint Stock Company and Civil Service have silently brought the salaried class into power', Keynes wrote in 1934.[27]

It was through the forging of a new relationship between the civil service and the joint stock companies that Keynes expected the 'socialisation of investment' to come about. He never supposed that the prince, in his modern guise of congeries of competing politicians, had divested himself of all private interest. That is why he supported Beveridge's proposal for an Economic General Staff: 'We shall never enjoy prosperity again', he wrote, 'if we continue indefinitely without some deliberate machinery for mitigating the consequences of selecting our governors on account of their gifts of oratory and

their power of detecting in good time which way the mind of unin-
structed opinion is blowing.'[28] Similarly, Keynes argued before the
Macmillan Committee that the principles of central banking should
and could be 'utterly removed from popular controversy and . . .
regarded as a kind of beneficient technique of scientific control such
as electricity or other branches of science are' – which prompted one
of his fellow commissioners to remark, 'You are a very sanguine
man'.[29]

On the other side, Keynes saw the public service motive growing
at the industrial level through the emergence of the 'semi-autonomous' corporation: in 1927 he estimated that two thirds of the
capital of large-scale undertakings could not be classed as private
any more.[30] The central thread of his argument had to do with the
tendency of large-scale industry to 'socialise' itself. By this he meant
the divorce of management from ownership, and the transformation
of the money-making into the 'public service' motive. He wrote of
'the trend of the Joint Stock Institutions, when they have reached a
certan age and size, to approximate to the status of the public
corporations rather than that of individualistic private enterprise.'[31]
Keynes welcomed these developments as ridding capitalism of its
'casino' features, while avoiding the dead hand of bureaucratic governmental controls. Interestingly, while left-wing commentators saw
in this concentration of private capital a powerful argument for
public ownership, Keynes believed it made it unnecessary, since the
'managers' were no longer short-term profit maximisers. The same
argument was later to be used by Anthony Crosland.[32] If large-scale
industry was already 'socialised', public ownership was superfluous.

The final assumption which underlay Keynes's vision of the
political economy of the future was that all these different parts of
the state would be controlled by much the same kind of people. The
'semi-autonomous' corporations would be run neither by cabinet
ministers nor by town councils but by boards chosen for business
ability, adequately remunerated, and free from bureaucratic interference. 'I do not see', he wrote 'why we should not build up in this
country a great public service running the business side of public
concerns recruited from the whole population with the same ability
and the same great tradition as our administrative Civil Service'.[33]
Keynes undoubtedly saw the 'socialisation' of large parts of the
economy, in the form of legally private, but public-spirited, corporations, run by university high-fliers and generating their own invest-

ment funds as providing the essential guarantee of a stable high level of investment; since it was this development which would mitigate the large-scale *fluctuations* of investment associated with the psychology of the stock market. Monetary fine-tuning and residual fiscal policy would be in the hands of different members of the same élite at the Bank of England and the Treasury. Thus he saw science, expertise, and public spirit gradually ousting politics and self-interest as governors of a system which remained largely unchanged in its legal, institutional forms.

Keynes's intellectual and managerial élitism left little room for what we would now call participatory democracy. In a revealing passage from a speech to the Liberal Summer School of 1925 (left out in the printed version published in his *Essays in Persuasion*) he stated his 'fundamental' objection to the Labour Party:

> I believe that the right solution [to the economic question] will involve intellectual and scientific elements which must be above the heads of the vast mass of more or less illiterate voters. Now, in a democracy, every party alike has to depend on this mass of ill-understanding voters . . . Nevertheless there are differences between the several parties in the degree to which the party machine is democratised in its details. In this respect the Conservative Party is in much the best position. The inner ring of the party can almost dictate the details and technique of policy. Traditionally the management of the Liberal Party was also sufficiently autocratic. Recently there have been ill-advised movements in the directon of democratising the party programme . . . The Labour Party, on the other hand, is in a far weaker position. I do not believe that the intellectual elements in the party will ever exercise adequate control; too much will always be decided by those who do not know *at all* what they are talking about . . .[34]

(4) Keynes and Socialism

There is little in Keynes's ethical or political beliefs which is distinctively socialist and much that is anti-socialist. It is not difficult to imagine him supporting the 'enlightened' Conservatism of Macmillan and Butler in the 1950s: indeed, he once remarked that it was the task of the Liberal Party to provide the Labour Party with ideas and the Conservatives with cabinets. But we must remember that for a Liberal of Keynes's generation, the Conservative Party was the historic enemy, and remained so throughout the inter-war years, despite the 'decency' of Stanley Baldwin. It was the party of stupidity and prejudice, standing pat on the old ways, and he habitually wrote about it in these terms, e.g., it 'ought to be concerning itself with evolving a version of individualistic capitalism adapted to the progressive change of circumstances. The difficulty is that the capitalist leaders in the City and in parliament are incapable of distinguishing novel measures for safeguarding capitalism from what they call Bolshevism.'[35] The other problem with the Conservatives was that they were the guardians of the reactionary codes of morals against which Keynes was in revolt: he could no more look to them to support 'scientific' birth control than 'scientific' monetary control, though there is nothing specifically 'socialist' about these things.

With the historical Liberal Party in decline, Keynes came to see the Labour Party as the most plausible vehicle of the reforms he wanted. In most of his political writings he is engaged in a dialogue with the Labour movement. This involved him in very ambiguous use of language as he tried at one and the same time to distinguish his position from that of socialism and also to stress the compatibility between liberal and socialist aspirations.

Keynes had three fundamental objections to socialism as he understood it. First, he challenged the doctrine that socialism was the only remedy for the ills of *laissez-faire*. He objected to it, that is, as a mechanism for securing economic reform on the grounds that its doctrines were ideological, obsolete, irrelevant, inimical to wealth-creation and likely to involve gross interferences with individual freedom. State socialism, he wrote in 1926, 'misses the significance of what is actually happening . . . There is, for instance, no so-called important political question so really unimportant, so irrelevant to the reorganisation of economic life in Britain as the nationalisation of the railways.'[36]

Secondly, Keynes objected to socialism's stress on the class basis of politics and thought: 'I can be influenced by what seems to me to be justice and good sense; but the class war will find me on the side of the educated bourgeoisie.'[37] Against the class analysis of socialists he always emphasised the importance of individual choice and character; the role of intelligence (Keynes only really recognised one class war: between the clever and the stupid); the autonomy of ideas; and the potential harmony of interests between capitalists and workers. These were the classic liberal positons.

Finally, Keynes did not believe in equality as an ethical or

political goal. He believed in equality of opportunity, but thought
that this state of affairs already largely existed in the England of his
day. (See above p.76). As for social justice, although Elizabeth
Johnson goes too far when she writes that it 'existed [for Keynes]
only in there not being enough jobs to go round',[38] his redistributionary aims were largely confined to limiting the incomes from the
lending of money.

Keynes's hostility to Marx and Marxism is too well-known to
require extensive quotation: 'Marxist Socialism', he declared in his
Sidney Ball lecture of 1924, 'must always remain a portent to the historians of thought – how a doctrine so illogical and so dull can have
exercised so powerful and enduring an influence over the minds of
men and, through them, the events of history.'[39] He believed that his
General Theory would 'knock away' the intellectual foundations of
Marxism.[40] Yet the similarities between Marx and Keynes are worth
exploring: their joint belief that capitalism was a stage in history that
would end when capital was plentiful; their moral and aesthetic distaste for the 'money-motive'; the resemblance of their Utopias.

Despite his contempt for socialism as a system of ideas, Keynes
was always careful to endorse a certain range of socialist ideals. The
atheist who thought Christianity a lot of 'hocus-pocus' sympathised
in 1925 with the 'religious' appeal of communism, so superior to the
'money-making' purposes which was all that western capitalism had
to offer.[41] The author of *The General Theory* could declare in 1939
that 'there is no one in politics today worth sixpence outside the
ranks of liberals except the post-war generation of intellectual communists under thirty-five'.[42] The mandarin civil servant had little
difficulty in subscribing to the Fabian ideal of public service. The
well-endowed Cambridge aesthete looked forward to the abolition
of the 'money motive' (Keynes never used the phrase 'profit motive')
as the basis of human activity.

Yet the main characteristic of the political writings Keynes
addressed to socialists is the separation between the present and the
future. Managed capitalism ('what is economically sound') is for
now; what Keynes calls 'socialism' ('what is economically unsound')
is for later – once the economic problem has been solved. The only
real bridge he offers is the growth of the 'public service' motive in
capitalism's womb – which means that actual public ownership is
not needed.[43] By these means Keynes set out to woo – and tame –
the Left.

(5) The Keynesian Logic of Intervention

The Keynesian revolution in economic policy was a particular manifestation of the general trend towards collectivism which distinguished the first half of this century from the first half of the nineteenth century. Its success derives from the fact that it offered a logic of collective action within the framework of liberal democracy. It did not raise in acute form issues which liberal democracy cannot easily handle – distributional questions, questions of property rights, questions about the relationship between liberty and legal coercion. The Keynesian logic of intervention offered the benefits of collectivism without any of its costs.

Collectivism is the belief that individual and/or social well-being cannot be achieved by individuals pursuing their own interests within the law but must be willed and brought about by the action of collective bodies, embodying the 'common will' of their members. The dominant forces behind the collectivist surge in our century are generally taken to be: the quest for economic security by individuals, firms, trades unions, and states; the quest for social and/or national efficiency; efforts to control the abuse of private power; and the quest for justice between classes. Twentieth-century collectivism has ranged all the way from centrally planned, owned, and politically controlled economies to milder forms of planning and selective public provision of goods and services which have been advocated not only as good in themselves but as inoculations against the more virulent forms of the disease.

Keynes was certainly a collectivist in the latter sense, but of a very precise kind. 'I come next', he wrote in 1924, 'to a criterion of the *Agenda* which is particularly relevant to what is urgent and desirable to do in the near future. We must aim at separating those services which are *technically social* from those which are *technically individual*. The most important *Agenda* of the State relate not to those activities which private individuals are already fulfilling, but to those functions which fall outside the sphere of the individual, to those decisions which are made by *no one* if the State does not make them. The important thing for government is not to do things which individuals are doing already, and to do them a little better or a little worse; but to do those things which at present are not done at all.' Examples of the agenda of government were (i) control of the business cycle by the central bank, (ii) control of the amount of savings and their flow as between domestic and foreign uses, and (iii) population policy, including attention to 'quality' as well as to mere numbers.[44]

The main charge against *laissez-faire* capitalism was not that private self-interest allocated resources inefficiently or unjustly as between different uses – Keynes specifically denies that it does[45] – but that it failed to ensure full use of the potential resources. This suggested a quite different logic of intervention from that of the reigning socialist and national socialist models, directed as they were to 'planning' for efficiency or national power, or the achievement of distributional justice.

Pre-Keynesian economics had no theory capable of explaining persisting mass unemployment. The fact of such unemployment was attributed to contractual, institutional, or legislative obstacles to the formation of market-clearing prices for labour. The only advice economists had to offer governments was to remove these obstacles, so that the institutional setting would once more be 'appropriate' for the achievement of full employment. Governments naturally shrank from dismantling most of the social and trade union legislation they had passed in the previous fifty years.

Keynes's earliest analysis of the unemployment problem – in terms of fluctuations in the quantity of money – had the great political merit of bypassing this set of problems. Given the institutional setting, and particularly the wages policies of employers and unions, the quantity of employment depended (within limits) on the quantity of money supplied by the central bank. If the operations of the gold standard prevented the central bank from supplying the appropriate quantity of money, then it should be jettisoned in favour of the 'labour standard', which would be maintained by varying the exchange rate.

Keynes clearly thought it was good economics to tackle unemployment on the least-cost principle. 'When we have got unemployment down to 4 or 5 per cent', he declared in 1924, 'then there are other causes which also have to be tackled by other methods, but, if you have the financial factor responsible for the difference (say) between 5 and 12 per cent, then . . . it is a matter well worth bending our energies to get rid of.'[46] Behind every monetary radical, as Galbraith has acutely remarked, lurks a social conservative. Behind Keynes's concentration on the monetary factor as a cause of unemployment lay a great deal of institutional timidity; he often expressed the view that an old, inflexible economy like England's could not take the classical medicine without the risk of grave social disorder.

Although in Keynes's mature theory the quantity of employment was made to depend (again within limits) on the level of demand (particularly investment demand) rather than on the quantity of money, prevention and cure remained, at least for shallow fluctuations of market demand, the task of monetary policy. Collectivism is confined to two points: provision by the central bank of an appropriate quantity of money, and by the state of an appropriate level of investment. Nothing else is to change. In the mature Keynes, the picture of a sluggishly self-healing economy has given way to one in which an economy experiencing a decline in investment-demand if left to itself, subsides into a state of permanent illness. Yet Keynes remained confident that a change in ideas superimposed on a natural evolution towards corporatism could cure the disease without any need for institutional change.

(6) Conclusion

Both Keynes's economic research programme and the way he 'modelled' the unemployment problem can be said to have been influenced by his ethical and political values in two ways, one negative, the other positive.

On the negative side, it was important that he did not come to economics with a prior commitment to achieving social justice through economic reform. As we have pointed out, his ethical commitments were personal, and were not importantly related to economics or politics. That is to say, his commitment to the civilised ideal did not imply any particular political or economic order. This meant that he had no initial bias towards seeing the unemployment problem as an effect of an unjust social order, as was general among thinkers on the Left. A comparison with J.A. Hobson, whom Keynes came to admire, is illuminating at this point. The weakness in Hobson's analysis, according to Keynes, was that he lacked an 'independent theory of the rate of interest', leading him to place too much emphasis on under-consumption, to be cured by redistributing wealth and income from the rich to the poor.[47] For Hobson, economic analysis had to be adapted to ethical commitment. The one important case with Keynes where ethical and economic values come into (somewhat tortured) relationship concerns the role of the rentier, an ethical type whom Keynes disliked and to whose 'euthanasia' he looked forward.

On the positive side is Keynes's political utilitarianism, as influenced by Burke and also by his own theory of probability. This led him to emphasise the connection between economic prosperity and political contentment/social order. But at the same time it was the 'happiness of our contemporaries' that he chiefly sought. He was not prepared to risk too much of the present for the sake of a better future, since 'our powers of prediction are too slight'. This insti-tutional timidity was reinforced by the rise of communism and fascism. However, Keynes's theory of probability gave him a justifi-cation for breaking with Moore's moral and Burke's political conservatism, since it purported to show how individuals and governments could, within a short time-range, act rightly for the right (rational) reasons. From this followed his preference for dis-cretion over rules; and his faith in intelligence and the rule of experts. He felt that industrial and political evolution was on the side of this development, by making markets in capital and politics less important. The economy would be stabilised by being 'social-ised', which meant that it did not have to be nationalised.

It remains to consider what is left of Keynes's political legacy today. Is it depleted beyond replenishment? Or does it still have the power to invigorate our thinking? Keynes raises in a variety of ways the central political question of our time, and perhaps all times: what we think a 'central authority' can or should do to bring about a more desirable state of affairs. Three issues deserve particular attention.

The first concerns the relationship between goodness and utility and more generally between ethics and politics. The classical tradition, which runs deep, is that politics is a means to, and part of, the 'good society'. Political utilitarianism broke finally with this by seeing government as a mere contrivance to satisfy certain wants. But much political practice, and the political vocation itself, rests on the older assumption. People may go into politics because they are ambitious, or because they feel that government should be as competent as possible; but they normally feel the need to justify their choice by saying that they aim to 'do good'. SDP militants, for example, feel that the party lacks 'ideals'; yet the SDP was formed, in part, to preserve the mixed economy. Keynes's political thought is for the cool hour, when politicians ask themselves what they really think they are doing, rather than for the platform where they trumpet their faiths.

The second issue concerns the relationship between élites and masses. Keynes's thinking challenges the ideal of a participatory democracy – whether in the form of consumer sovereignty which the Right offers or in the form of popular decision making advocated by the Left. Keynes clearly saw conflict between direct government and good government; and while he would not have denied the educative value of popular democracy, he would not have taken too many risks for what would be at best a long-run benefit. It may be we are in a position to go further than Keynes by taking into account different levels of decision making: direct democracy may be appropriate in some places and not in others. A related question is this: if Keynes was wrong in thinking that certain kinds of high-level decision making could be insulated from vested interest or vote-catching how does this affect our judgement about the proper sphere of public action? Is the Prince inevitably and irretrievably tainted by corruption? Or is he our main safeguard against it?

Thirdly, there is the relationship between management and reform. Keynes's approach, and that of his generation of liberals, was heavily infected by institutional timidity. This gave a 'demand-side' bias to his economics, which became even more pronounced in the post-war Keynesian régime. Have we now reached the end of this road? Keynes saw institutional reform as fraught with danger for social stability. Moreover, he saw institutions evolving in a manner helpful to his macro-economic purposes. But to what extent is institutional reform, in Britain today and in the near future, a necessary condition of fuller employment? To put it concretely: are the wage-determining and political institutions such that any Keynesian policy is bound to generate, at an early date, unacceptable levels of inflation? It may be that reform has become a less risky option than reliance on unaided management, though management will still be needed. Keynesian liberalism, in other words, may need some of the cutting edge of an earlier, less embattled, liberalism, if good government is to be preserved.

Notes

I would like to thank the following for comments on an earlier version of this paper: Mrs Jean Floud; Professor Partha Das Gupta; Dr Larry Siedentop; the Political Theory Group at the University of Warwick; the SDP Political Philosophy Group.

DISCUSSION ON SIX

In discussion, Keynes's 'institutional timidity' aroused considerable interest. It seemed clear that Keynes thought the traditional institutions adequate to solving the economic and employment problems, provided they were properly managed by a disinterested élite. It also appeared that Keynes's 'somewhat comprehensive socialisation of investment' depended likewise on the management of public corporations by this same élite in the public interest, making nationalisation superfluous. He was not much interested in democracy except as an educative process; though a lifelong Liberal, he had none of the passion for participatory democracy of J.S. Mill.

One of the main weaknesses of this approach, it was suggested, was that neither Keynes nor his followers had any theory of the state. It was to be presumed, as Robert Skidelsky had said, that by the state Keynes meant 'that sector of the polity, not working for private self-interest but for the public good'. This cut across the public/private sector divide and included bodies which were legally private but had evolved in such a way as to acquire some sense of public purpose. The inadequacy of this lay in the assumption that the state, thus loosely defined, would simply take on new functions without changing its character. Exactly the same assumption was made by the democratic socialists in the 1930s; Evan Durbin and co also thought that a planning team of high-flying Oxbridge graduates could do the job, and no deeper thought on the purpose or character of the state was required.

Responding to this, Robert Skidelsky recalled that the pre-1939 theories of the powerful benevolent state, though adopted by the Left, were in fact originated by fascists (Giovanni Gentile, etc.). It was partly in reaction to this that the Austrian liberal economists had developed a powerful anti-state theory, which was carried still further by Buchanon and other neo-liberals of the Virginia school. All this contributed in a very significant way to the failure of Keynes and other twentieth-century intellectuals to develop a convincing theory of the state, or a convincing critique of the political process.

The point was made that political powers had to be

'earthed' to keep them limited. For Hobbes the state itself could decide what its functions should be, but this was unacceptable to democrats: we could not allow the state to define its own functions. Yet, this was the actual position in Britain today. If the power of the state was to be limited, there must be clear criteria for this limitation and for deciding which public goods were to be publicly provided.

On the economic side, the view was advanced that Keynes, like many other Oxbridge mandarin types, had little interest in wealth creation; in contrast to Schumpeter he preferred the don and the judge to the capitalist. But our great present difficulty was that we were trying to promote social democracy in a country with a particularly run-down economy. How could one reconcile Keynesian attitudes with the nineteenth-century Anglo-American tradition which kept the state out of the economy, leaving it to the market to take care of growth? It was pointed out here that the long-term growth path of the British economy had only been about 2% over the century 1870-1970, so the low-growth trend was there long before Keynes came on the scene.

On the question whether it was possible to derive a 'right to employment' from Keynes's 'Lockean' liberalism, on the grounds that for Locke employment was a surrogate for property, there was some hesitation in the group. But there was no doubt whatever that Keynes saw full employment as a 'public good' and believed, as Robert Skidelsky had suggested, that it should be tackled on the least-cost principle in the interests of social stability.

In his paper Robert Skidelsky had concluded that Keynes's political legacy was to raise in a variety of ways the central political issue of our time, and probably of all time, i.e. what a 'central authority' could or should do to bring about a more desirable state of affairs. Owing to his 'institutional timidity' Keynes's own preference was for management over reform. But it now looked as if reform might well be a less risky option that unaided management. We could and should be more radical than Keynes was prepared to be; we could now afford to experiment more boldly, since democratic institutions were no longer under such real threat as they had been in the inter-war period. This left us in search of a new model for liberalism. Accordingly, it was decided to look next across the Atlantic at developments in American liberalism. John Rawls is a philosopher who has excited a good deal of interest among British social democrats. Inigo Bing and Kevin Carey had recently devoted a Tawney Society pamphlet to a study of Rawls and agreed to contribute the paper that follows.

SEVEN

John Rawls and American Liberalism

INIGO BING AND KEVIN CAREY

The essence of liberalism is freedom of choice. There may be dis-
agreements about how this is realised; about how much the state
needs to intervene to make that freedom a reality for individuals,
about where the line is drawn between freedom and social responsibility, but there is no argument about the core philosophy; liberal
social and political institutions exist to allow individuals to live
their lives according to their own interpretation of what 'the good
life' is.

Selling this idea to voters in Britain is peculiarly difficult because
they believe that they have this freedom already and do not need
politicians calling themselves liberals making an issue about protecting it. These voters rightly understand that they have chosen their
own political view – conservatism or socialism – without interference from anyone and they regard any talk of possible dictatorship
or curtailment of rights as scaremongering.

In Britain the irony for the liberal is acute; he is the heir to a
political system which enables class-based politics to survive and
prosper. He lives in a country known throughout the world for its
'liberal institutions' even though, as Marx rightly diagnosed, it has
been a cockpit of class-based politics since the dawn of the Industrial Revolution. Living in a country without a bill of rights, where
50% plus one of the House of Commons can make or unmake any
law they please without let or hindrance, the liberal knows that the
survival of free institutions depends on the fragile basis of honour
rather than on the solid basis of constitutional rights.

Exercising freedom of choice becomes more difficult as the
number of available choices increases and so the irony for the liberal
deepens. The more choice he provides through his advocacy, the
more people shy away from the difficulty of choosing, and seek
refuge in political theories that provide answers through their
various definitions of 'the good life' which they wish to impose on

society through the use of liberal political institutions.

In the United States, on the other hand, liberalism has fared much better. Its written constitution is the finest product of eighteenth-century liberalism and the history of its politics has revolved around the two questions implied in the opening paragraph of this essay – how far does the enjoyment of rights under a liberal constitution require government intervention, particularly in the economic and welfare sphere, and what constraints may society as a whole place on individual conduct? Government intervention in economic and social matters and freedom from social restraint in individual conduct both reached their zenith in Johnson's completion of the Kennedy programme. Then came the backlash.

The 'new right' or 'moral majority', correctly saw liberalism as quintessentially permissive, as a threat to the universal acceptance of its definition of 'the good life'; it wanted to replace economic and social paternalism and moral independence with economic and social independence and moral paternalism. The radicals, on the other hand, thought that government intervention in economic and social matters had not gone far enough, particularly in enabling women and minorities to enjoy their constitutional rights. Worse still, a 'liberal' government was actively involved in the Vietnam war which was morally indefensible in itself and whose cost delayed improvements at home.

Liberalism, therefore, faced an attack on two fronts, and what might have started as differences of judgement on single policies broadened into an attack on fundamental liberal principles.

In view of what has already been noted concerning the essentially passive characteristics of liberalism, its counterattack was surprisingly swift and assertive. It was theoretically impressive and studiously concrete.

First, John Rawls in *A Theory of Justice*[1] provided a framework in which liberty and equality were seen as mutually reinforcing rather than conflicting. Then, from the egalitarian perspective, Ronald Dworkin in *Taking Rights Seriously*[2] and *A Matter of Principle*[3] showed how the root principle of liberalism was equality.

Undoubtedly *A Theory of Justice* made the greatest initial impact and will have the greatest long-term influence. Dworkin, on the other hand, carries Rawls's arguments from their Olympian (and sometimes Delphic) plane into the everyday world of difficult decisions.

The views in *A Theory of Justice* have their foundation in the contract theories of John Locke, owe much to the concepts of liberty
espoused by John Stuart Mill and have important new insights on
equality which was a dominant concern of the early Fabians and
a consuming passion of social democrats such as R.H. Tawney.
John Rawls is a philosopher of immense scholarship but he became
of interest to politicians because he tried to demonstrate that there
was such a thing as justice which underlined our moral and political
outlook. He argued that not only could justice be revealed and
explained but that it could be a foundaton for political institutions.

A Theory of Justice is based on two principles. The first principle
is that each person is to have an equal right to the most extensive
total system of basic liberties compatible with a similar system of
liberty for all. (Such liberties are: political liberty – the right to vote
and be eligible for public office, freedom of speech and assembly;
liberty of conscience and freedom of thought; freedom of the person
and the right to hold personal property; and freedom from arbitrary
arrest and seizure as defined by the rule of law.)

The second principle is that social and economic inequalities are
to be arranged so that they are both (a) to the greatest advantage to
the least advantaged, consistent with the just savings principle,* and
(b) attached to offices and positions open to all under the conditions
of fair equality of opportunity.[4]

These are the principles which 'free and rational persons
concerned to further their own interest would accept in an initial
position of equality as defining the fundamental terms of their
association'.[5] Rawls stresses that this is an agreement, arrived at in a
hypothetical situation where the 'specific contingencies' of ordinary
life are excluded.

Rawls calls this the 'original position' where people exist under a
'veil of ignorance' which can be described as follows: imagine a congress of human beings; they are not yet a society but have agreed to
construct together some principles for living alongside one another

---

*. The just savings principle arises because of the problem of justice between
generations. Each generation must not only preserve its own gains, it must
also put something aside for capital accumulation. The saving is just if there
is an understanding between generations as to how the burdens and benefits
of realising and preserving a just society are to be shared. This theoretical
understanding constrains the immediate application of the second principle,
hence the formulation 'consistent with the just savings principle'.

in a civilised and peaceful manner. Unfortunately, these people have one huge disadvantage. No one knows his or her social status, intelligence, race or inheritance. Nor do any of them know what cultural or economic condition the society will be in when they have formed it or whether, when it has been formed, they will be rich or poor, talented or stupid, physically strong or mentally disabled. They must do the best they can under this 'veil of ignorance'. All they have is a generalised knowledge of political affairs, the principles of economic theory, the basis of social organisation, and the laws of human psychology. They know also that any decision they take is for all time – binding therefore on future generations – and that there will be no second chance to re-write the principles.

The two principles are ranked in what Rawls calls 'lexical order', so that in any conflict between economic efficiency and the claim of liberty justified by the first principle, the claim of liberty must prevail. His theory is not affected by the obvious point that the liberty of the newspaper editor to freedom of expression is greater than, say, the unemployed carpenter's liberty to freedom of expression. The reason is that one must not confuse the 'worth of liberty' with the 'value of liberty'. The value of liberty to the unemployed carpenter is the same as for the editor even though the former will not be able to exercise his liberty in the same way.

Rawls's insistence on the priority of liberty owes much to J.S. Mill. *On Liberty* was written in 1859, and was itself clearly influenced by de Tocqueville's massive work *Democracy in America*. Both books described and defined the principles which the emerging democracies in Britain and the United States might threaten. John Stuart Mill described liberty not as a licence to do what one likes irrespective of its effect on others, but liberty as self-government, meaning that each person was equal and independent. Such independence was for Mill an aspect of equality because a person's independence was threatened not only by a political system that denied him an equal voice, but also by political decisions which denied him equal respect.

Mill's views were highly influential, although as socialism gradually replaced liberalism as the dominant progressive philosophy in Britain it became commonplace to assume there was a conflict between equality and liberty which involved constant trade-offs between one and the other. One of Rawls's most telling arguments is that equality is the basis for preserving and extending liberties and that the fundamental right to treatment as an equal requires basic liberties. He explains why liberty and equality ought not to conflict in the following way:

> Some writers have distinguished between equality as it is invoked in connection with the distribution of certain goods, some of which will almost certainly give higher status or prestige to those who are more favoured, and equality as it applies to the respect which is owed to persons irrespective of their social position. Equality of the first kind is defined by the second principle of justice which regulates the structure of organisations and distributive shares so that social co-operation is both efficient and fair. But equality of the second kind is fundamental. It is defined by the first principle of justice and by such natural duties as that of mutual respect: it is owed to human beings as moral persons.[6]

Rawls devotes a complete section of his book to explaining why his principles express an 'egalitarian conception of justice', and his views on the egalitarian basis of liberty are trenchantly summed up by Ronald Dworkin:

> Rawls's most basic assumption is not that men have a right to certain liberties that Locke or Mill thought important, but that they have a right to equal respect and concern in the design of political institutions . . . it cannot be denied in the name of any more radical concept of equality because none exists.[7]

It is clear therefore that Rawls upholds liberty, self-interest, mutual respect and equality as defining the 'just' society, and it is these concepts which lead Rawls to his famous and vehement refutation of utilitarianism. Rawls maintains that any distribution must be designed to further an *individual's* best interests, and therefore it is necessary to identify those interests which are fundamental, and therefore non-negotiable, in any distribution. The utilitarian on the other hand argues that improving average welfare is fundamental and that resources and benefits must be distributed to that end.

Rawls answers Henry Sidgwick's formulation of utilitarianism ('a society is rightly ordered and therefore just when its major institutions are arranged so as to achieve the greatest net balance of satisfaction summed over all the individuals belonging to it'[8]) in the following way: 'It hardly seems likely that persons who view themselves as equals, entitled to press their claims upon one another, would agree to a principle which may require lesser life prospects for some simply for the sake of a greater sum of advantages enjoyed by others.'[9] Second he argues that utilitarianism blunts self-esteem, confidence and pride in one's own worth, and relies too heavily on altruism and benevolence to achieve justice rather than mutual concern and respect.

The concept of 'average utility' is too blunt an instrument for assessing individual needs, and utilitarians are too preoccupied with consequences to society rather than concerns of individuals whose happiness is of instrumental, not intrinsic, importance. The utilitarian reasoning which equates rights only with corresponding duties would mean excluding freedom of conscience because there is no reciprocal duty associated with this fundamental liberty.

The utilitarian's defence against this logical assault is to say that notwithstanding its defects it is the only feasible and workable way of achieving equality because the maxim 'everybody to count for one and nobody for more than one' is the best we can do to ensure justice for all. It is the demolition of the utilitarian's arguments for equality that is one of Rawls's most impressive achievements. If it is indeed true that everybody is to count for one and nobody for more than one in the distribution of resources and the making of choices, then utilitarianism could claim that the principle of treating each person with equal concern and respect is fulfilled. The problem is that any such choices are nearly always made for reasons which are *personal*, affecting one's own preferences, and *external*, affecting the consequences on others.

Thus I may personally prefer private medical health care, in order to be treated quickly, and believe that if I am treated privately a health service bed will become available for someone else. My choice has been shown to be personal and external. If, however, the majority in a community are in a position to afford private care and a minority not, then if the majority believe the community will be generally better off by the exercise of their own choice, the minority have not been accorded an equal concern and respect in the design of health resources. It is in the self-interest of the minority to have as good a provision of health care as the majority who can afford private medicine, but the rights of the minority in this example cannot be satisfied on utilitarian principles.[10]

The egalitarian nature of Rawls's arguments leads strongly to the conclusion that a right to treatment as an equal is a central pivot of a just society. This concept is sometimes but not always the same as equal treatment. Thus a disabled person may be denied a university place on the grounds of ability, intelligence, motivation and so on, but if he is granted a place he must be treated as an equal with able-bodied students even if this means redesigning access to public buildings or reproducing books in braille. The idea that equal liberty has a priority and may only be reduced for the sake of liberty would apply to arguments over censorship and the enforcement of morality. One cannot, on liberal principles, ban violence on television simply because a non-violent society is a desirable goal, but only if by showing the programme there would be a still worse invasion of liberty. Such an invasion would include subliminal advertising which would threaten a free exercise of choice or an obvious debasement of children whose self-respect would be infringed.

Rawls is therefore careful not to describe a just society in terms of goals, but rather in terms of the *rights* of individuals to personal fulfilment, mutual respect and the equal sharing of fundamental liberties. The second, or Difference Principle, which deals with distribution, follows logically from the first. Two things may distort natural competition and fulfilment on equal terms. First, accidents of birth, inheritance or geographical location may make it inherently impossible for an individual to compete fairly with his neighbour. Second, the contribution made by a person in society may deny him the mutual respect and concern from others that he might otherwise enjoy. Rawls does not favour eliminating these differences, but he wishes to see that no one gains or loses from his arbitrary place in the distribution of natural assets or his own position in society without giving or receiving compensating advantages in return.

It is not a *goal* of equality which leads Rawls to the Difference Principle, because he regards it as a natural fact that some people will be born into society in different circumstances from others, and these undeserved inequalities do not call for 'redress' or a *requirement* that society irons them out. Undeserved inequalities involve a recognition that those who benefit from them can only do so if thereby the condition of the worse-off is also improved.

Rawls is therefore not only anti-utilitarian, he is also anti-socialist in the commonly understood sense of the term because the socialist concept of equality – equality of outcome – *does* embody the principle of redress. The Difference Principle, on the other hand, deals with undeserved *inequalities*, and these would be worse if the

Difference Principle were not satisfied.

Rawls accepts that much of life is unfair, but that in a just society self-respect will be reciprocated, and fraternity ('the idea of not wanting to have greater advantages unless this is to the benefit of others who are less well off') will flourish. In this way it is argued that the Difference Principle is mutually supportive: the better-off enjoy a system where their talents and self-esteem can advantage them, while contributing 'as moral persons' to a just society, while the worse-off are benefited because without the Difference Principle they would be even worse off.

The Difference Principle is therefore a rather minimalist notion of social justice; it fails to deal with inequalities which arise between citizens operating in the market who are not right at the bottom of the social and economic ladder. Rawls's statement of his two principles appears to found redistribution firmly on the second principle; but Dworkin shows that the basis of social and economic equality lies in the full implementation of the first principle; the second principle merely deals with any inequalities which remain after the full recognition of the first principle.

Dworkin does not see inequalities arising merely because people in a general sense are different and can never be the same but rather because even with equal strength in the market, guaranteed by their being accorded equal concern and respect in the distribution of resources, they will choose to use what they have in different ways. It is not for the state to impose equality at all times in all circumstances just because one man has taken a risk where another has been cautious or where one man has chosen to be relatively idle while another has chosen to sacrifice his leisure in the pursuit of greater income. The problem with equality of outcome is that it fails to take into account what citizens put into society as well as what they take out.

There are many reasons why Rawls's ideas should be of interest to social democrats. He provides cogent reasons why the achievement of a just and fair society is not the exclusive preserve of socialists. His central contentions about individual rights is obviously attractive to a party which wants to introduce a bill of rights, and the doctrine of equal concern and respect is crucial to a party which believes in complete sexual and racial equality. The arguments for the priority of liberty powerfully uphold the case for tolerance in personal morality, and undermine the self-serving or the curtailment of personal freedom used by Marxists and conservatives.

But there is a final and even more powerful case for justice as fairness. If Britain is badly divided and ill-governed under our political system, as social democrats contend, then there can be no consensus as to what *average utility* is. Utilitarianism may work if it is clear what maximising average utility involves, but it is doubtful if there is such agreement in Britain today. As social democrats have frequently argued, a change in the system is as important as the creation of new policies.

Rawls and Dworkin are clear about the constitutional arrangements required by 'justice as fairness' but Dworkin, in clarifying Rawls's attitude to economic arrangements, diverges from him and produces a liberal view of equality which requires the existence of the economic market and rejects a planned economy, where Rawls claims that justice as fairness could flourish in a capitalist or liberal socialist system.

For the liberal, constitutional arrangements are relatively straightforward. The state is established by contract to act as an agent on behalf of citizens. The contract must be recognised (its terms should be published), it should be balanced between citizen and state (fair and free elections should be held at reasonable intervals), its implementation should be open (through the publication of information), it should be predictable (not open to arbitrary interpretations). Further, provision must be made to ensure that the contract is fair to all citizens, that is, its terms should not be unfair to individuals even if such unfairness is advocated by a majority, and it should be subject to fundamental re-examination and change as social perceptions of justice become more refined.

The state starts out in its relations with citizens with an enormous advantage; government can, if it wishes, unilaterally break its contract, infringe the rights of citizens and quell any protest by wrongly using the power given to it. It can also, through its control of information, mislead citizens. Finally, and crucially, it can give itself power to keep the power it has. In a very real sense power is like a magnet, it attracts more power to it and finds it difficult to give up what it has acquired.

Much constitutional debate has revolved round the question of the duty of citizens to obey law and generally to demonstrate their sense of justice; certain right-wing political theorists have inherited the 'duty-based' constitutional outlook of the Middle Ages and made the duty of citizens the central constitutional issue. In this they have only differed from the far left as to the social goal which justifies the imposition of that duty on the citizen. There has been much less debate about the duty of the state, not least because of state power to dictate the political agenda, and also because those in power (the government) and those within reach of it (the opposition) are generally disposed to keep a system which is or is about to be to their respective advantage.

An examination of the British system yields depressing results. With the exception of the latent elective dictatorship enshrined in the 'sovereignty of parliament' the nature of the contract is vague because any specific proposals contained in law can be instantly overturned; following on from this, it is clear that citizens do not have basic rights, they are permitted by the government to do certain things until such time as the permission is withdrawn. There is no right to government information, which severely restricts the democratic process, while the political duopoly which has effectively operated until recently has severely limited the ability of the citizen to place matters of concern on the political agenda, particularly as both parts of the duopoly have agreed about the power of the state even though they have disagreed about the ends to which it should be applied.

In this situation the liberal would call for a written constitution, a bill of rights and a right to information. The justification for the first two is increasingly recognised if not yet universally accepted but the role of information in a democracy has been clouded, on the one hand by the notion of 'national security' and on the other by the belief that the relative independence of the BBC and the IBA and the existence of a 'free press' are satisfactory safeguards. Where freedom of information is concerned, the government should have to justify any withholding of information because disclosure would damage an identifiable individual, group, or the nation as a whole. A blanket appeal to national security is an inadequate explanation. As for the ability of the citizen to place items of concern on the political agenda, the current situation is far from satisfactory; the right to self-expression is theoretical but hardly practical. In this respect, the issue of broadcasting the House of Commons is not a matter of how such an action might affect the conduct or standing of the institution; it is a matter of prime constitutional importance. In an open democracy failure to broadcast the proceedings of the legislature is totally without justification.

Economic arrangements for the liberal are not so straightforward. His basic instinct is to opt for the market because this allows individual self-determination in a general way, but it is an imperfect mechanism because the individual's ability to operate in the market is limited by his own talents, his environment and his good or bad luck. The modern liberal is tempted, in recognising basic social and economic inequalities, to flirt with a more controlled economic environment where the state guarantees certain social and economic benefits. In this context, Dworkin identifies three different kinds of equality. He dismisses 'equality of opportunity' as meaningless, because nobody now opposes it in principle but many people do not enjoy it in practice. He regards equality of outcome as superficially attractive but dismisses this because it requires the state to give unequally to some citizens over others and to value certain goods and services more highly than others by providing them with subsidies. He opts, in conclusion, for 'equality of concern and respect', for the right of the citizen to have his concerns given equal weight by the government in decision-making. Where the market acts against the enjoyment by the citizen of roughly equal opportunity, the citizen can call upon rights which he holds as trump cards.[11] The market, plus these rights, is the best settlement which guarantees individual freedom while giving roughly equal strength to citizens in the market-place.

This analysis leads to some interesting conclusions for social democrats. First, there is the justification for negative income tax. Secondly, it directs the taxation system as a whole towards taxing what people take out of the economy rather than what they put into it, taxes on consumption rather than on saving. Thirdly, and stressed much more carefully by Rawls than by Dworkin, is a call for the curtailment of inherited income and wealth, which can only be justified in a system which does not guarantee the kind of equality called for by Rawls's first principle. Fourthly, equality of concern and respect demands that no citizen should have less of something just so that someone else can have more. Finally, over and above the provision of collective public goods such as clean air and defence, there is no reason why redistribution to give citizens equal strength within the democratic system and within the market should take the form of publicly provided, state-determined redistribution through such mechanisms as a national health service or a national education service. All citizens are *entitled* to education and health, but the way in which they acquire the enjoyment of these benefits is for them to decide.

The discussion of the role of the state with regard to economic matters has always been at the centre of politics, but in Britain that debate has become of crucial importance. On what basis has the state the right to demand sacrifices from its citizens and how should that sacrifice be apportioned? Dworkin in particular is emphatic that no citizen should be denied the allocation of resources to which equal concern and respect entitled him. He should not, for instance, be expected to accept unemployment now so that society in general might be better off either now or in the future. In any case, as Dworkin points out, the poor who make such sacrifices hardly ever benefit from them even in the long run and there are certain losses which can never be made up, such as psychological damage because of unemployment or malnutrition suffered in childhood. The citizen, recognising his own role in society, might make sacrifices which increase his self-esteem or the esteem in which society holds him, but in general those who make sacrifices, such as the person becoming unemployed through no fault of his own, as a direct result of government policy, is not regarded as a model citizen suffering for the general good, he is regarded as a layabout or scrounger, as a social parasite sapping the general well-being of society.

Far from incurring opprobrium for his misfortune, the citizen who makes a sacrifice for the general good is entitled to every assistance to minimise its consequences; the unemployed, for example, are entitled to retraining.

In the last two centuries there has been a belief in a mechanism which allowed anyone to exercise their own preferences while simultaneously advancing the 'general good'. Surely that grand utilitarian illusion has now been shattered; the advancement of the general good has always involved involuntary sacrifices by the least well off for the benefit of the better off. Utilitarianism is just a grand-sounding word for selfishness.

DISCUSSION ON SEVEN

Unsurprisingly, the sharp attack on utilitarianism mounted by Bing and Carey from their Rawlsian base-camp provoked lively discussion. They had suggested that utilitarianism relied too heavily on benevolence, altruism and social engineering by the state, implemented by a rational disinterested bureaucracy. Justice could only be achieved, however, by a rational pursuit of self-interest within a contractual framework such as that provided by Rawls's 'original position'. Rawls was scathing about benevolence.

In the discussion on Keynes it had been suggested that one of the weaknesses of liberalism was the lack of any modern theory of the state. This was now raised again in relation to Rawls: the state as such did not appear once in *A Theory of Justice*; there seemed to be a tacit assumption that the state was ethically neutral rather than being a power with distinct interests of its own, as was the case in Britain. Surely it was naive of Rawls to overlook this. It was admitted by Kevin Carey that Rawls was somewhat complacent about the state, which could in fact take three main forms: it could be rights-based, goals-based or duty-based. Rawls himself and Dworkin were firmly in the rights-based camp (which would of course, if accepted, lead to a neutral state). The trouble with utilitarianism was that it had to rely on a combination of goals (dependent on government action) and duty (dependent on altruism). The great thing about a rights-based system was that you decreased government power and you dispensed with altruism.

Against this it was pointed out that there was no rights-based tradition behind our system of government; we had abandoned that approach very early, possibly (as had been suggested in an earlier discussion) out of fright at the French Revolution, and it was difficult to see how we could get back on that course. Objection was also raised to rights deriving from self-interest based on the 'original position', as in the real world you started from a conjunction of circumstances which was nowhere near the 'original position', so you did need altruism if some people were going to give up some of the things they already had. Others were less worried about the 'original position' which they saw merely as a technical piece of methodology.

Rights continued to dominate the discussion: rights hadn't mattered much in the Middle Ages when all you were bothered about was whether you were going to heaven or hell. But they mattered now: the right to work was deeply embedded in Rawls; the right to information was vital; nobody in Britain was openly responsible for anything; such rights as we had depended on the whim of parliament. A reservation was expressed: one of the troubles about rights movements was that they tended to be fragmented and promoted by minority pressure groups often in conflict with one another. Those, it was cautioned, were *claims* rather than *rights*; rights by definition had to be general; the rights of the 'least advantaged' could not logically override others. A bill of rights, it was then argued, would subsume all other rights. But here we were warned that, though rights philosophers had had a very cutting edge in the nineteenth century, they now had a conservative tinge, aiming to entrench property rights against infringement by any Labour government; a bill of rights would also give an awful lot of power to judges; much could be done by recognising and implementing existing rights. Rawls and Dworkin, we were then reminded, thought individuals had prior existing rights; utilitarians did not – that was the great divide. All the same, rights within a utilitarian system could be recognised by their general utility; utilitarianism was perfectly compatible with 'a lean set of rights'.

The question was raised whether utilitarians would disagree with Rawls's second principle, namely that social and economic inequalities were to be arranged so that they were both reasonably likely to be to everyone's advantage and were attached to positions and offices open to all. Total utility could be compatible with redistribution from the better to the worse off. However, the caveat was entered here that utilitarianism could only be redistributive in a growth situation.

It was next asked where Rawls fitted into American politics. Was he taken up by Carter? Inigo Bing said that the German SPD was interested in Rawls and that civil disobedience had brought him into the North American political arena in the post-Vietnam period, when he was taken up by east coast intellectuals. It was also suggested that Gary Hart's programme had its roots in Rawls. It was not felt that Rawls's Americanness made him irrelevant – assuming an expanding economy and mobility of labour. But his contractual model, it was suggested, was undoubtedly more at home in the land of the founding fathers and a written constitution; Rawls belonged very much in the North American milieu.

Towards the end of this discussion it was objected that Rawls talked in a highly Lockean way of isolated individuals vis-à-vis a shadowy state; that what we wanted was a theory geared to justice and distribution in a more concrete society; and that we should be alive not only to the strengths but also to the weaknesses of very abstract models. As it was Dorothy Emmet who made these points, she was asked if she would develop her thoughts in a paper.

EIGHT

The Moral Roots
of Social Democracy

DOROTHY EMMET

The SDP pursues democratic politics with moral conviction. Can philosophy do anything to sharpen this? Moral philosophy is not monolithic; it contains a number of views, among them utilitarian, natural rights and social contract views. I am not going to present one of these as *the* moral theory of social democracy. Philosophical theories are perforce abstract and continually contested among philosophers. They define different ways of looking at moral questions, and emphasise different considerations to be taken into account in making moral judgements. Thus utilitarianism tells us to estimate consequences of courses of action as likely to contribute to some utility, currently generally called 'welfare' rather than the notoriously elusive happiness. Or it can be made a matter of maximising the satisfaction of preferences, without specifying what they are for. But there are well-known difficulties; for instance, as to how one weighs comparative utilities, and how one ranks the different preferences of different people. Mathematical attempts to deal with these questions do not, at any rate as yet, admit of widespread application. There is also the question of whether individuals have rights which should not be overridden for some aggregate general good. Rights theorists will say rights overtrump other considerations: but is this always so? And rights nowadays have a way of proliferating. Social contract views are attractive in making social morality a matter of rational agreement, but they make it appear as though a society could institute itself from scratch. Not one of these theories by itself is adequate to the complexities of social morality, and no one of them should be put forward as authoritative. So instead of presenting an overall theory, I shall look at some of the actual moral roots which can feed social democracy, and from which it can grow.

There are certain features which should characterise such a view:

1 It should not be utopian; that is to say, it should not presuppose a society a long way removed from our own, that being one in which people have various life styles, as well as conflicts in their moral outlooks. Moreover, as Burke said, a society is not 'a problem in arithmetic', so that one can solve it and draw a line under the answer. A society is a process where problems dealt with in one context come up again in new forms in others.

2 It should recognise that people have various motivations – not only that their motives can be mixed, but also that sustaining a democracy is so difficult that it needs to call on more than one kind of motive. In particular, we should avoid a simplistic choice between 'self-interest' and 'altruism' as a 'foundation'.

3 Though politics is not exclusively a matter of interests, it is largely so. Any view therefore has to take account of how our interests, and particularly our group interests, are likely to conflict, and how they can affect our moral outlook. Marx called this 'ideology'. It is not, I believe, the whole truth, but it contains truth that liberals in particular are tempted to underestimate.

4 Social and public morality is not the same as personal and private morality. Thus, the utilitarian aspect of reckoning consequences will generally be paramount in responsible public actions, whereas principle and sentiment may be more likely to be guiding lights in personal dealings. But there is no sharp dividing line. We have to be alert to likely consequences in private actions, and one might say that decisions on public actions should generally be made on utilitarian grounds by people who are not utilitarians, but who know the pull of principle and sentiment.

If we cannot deduce right public actions from an overall theory, this means there is no escape from the need for *judgement*. But if there is no one theory, there can nevertheless be an articulating of moral attitudes guiding our convictions, and this is where philosophy may come in.

Articulating fundamental attitudes and convictions is not the same as applying a simple model of moral democracy. A simple model may have its uses in bringing out some features of democracy. But it will omit others which can also be important. John Rawls's *Theory of Justice* is one such model, and it has been mooted as an appropriate philosophical view for the SDP. In my recent Tawney

Society pamphlet[1] I criticised Rawls on two grounds: (i) his model is highly abstract, whereas for a social contract to get going we have to presuppose an already existing community with understandings and practices; moreover, one should not expect to set up unchangeable institutions; (ii) his Principle of Difference, by which inequalities are justified if they are to the advantage of the worst-off, is a prudential self-interest view rather than a view of justice insofar as it appeals to a maximin strategy (where one makes the best provision for the worst outcome). This is because when making a rational choice under the 'veil of ignorance' we would not know whether we might not be in the least advantaged position, and so we would opt for a distribution which would make it as good for us as possible. In a recent paper,[2] *Justice as Fairness: Political not Metaphysical*, Rawls says that 'it was an error in *Theory* (and a misleading one) to describe a theory of justice as part of the theory of rational choice'; here he postulates not a maximin strategy, but autonomous, equal, and reasonable persons, with such moral qualities as make them willing to co-operate in democratic arrangements. Beyond this, he wants a democracy to be neutral as between people's 'good' and ways of life, provided these do not prevent them subscribing to the principles which define the democratic arrangements. (This would take care of the person whose 'good' might be to be a skilful cat burglar). So my criticism that this is a prudential view, rather than one of justice, need not now apply. I stand, however, by my contention about abstraction. A model of autonomous, equal, reasonable persons starting from scratch and agreeing on fair principles on which to co-operate is fine, but it is, as Rousseau said of democracy, a model 'for Gods and the sons of Gods'. I want to supplement this by a view closer to the ground, looking, to quote another tag of Rousseau's, at 'men as they are and institutions as they might be', and so I need a moral psychology with a thicker view of the kinds of motivation needed to make democracy tick. Rawls says that his view is not a moral psychology of motivation, but a postulate of the thinnest conditions needed for his model. So we are doing different things. This is not to say that if a model gives a few clear principles they cannot be valuable guides. Yet principles can conflict, and when they do, I do not believe they fall into a set hierarchy by which priorities can be settled. They are therefore necessary but not sufficient guides.

If social morality cannot be presented in a simple theory, neither can democracy. Democracy, as a form of political activity, is concerned with how a society is to be governed, and so with uses of power. Within a democracy power is held subject to popular support. Constitutional ways of registering this may be blunt instruments, but they allow different sets of people to be in power without resort to coups or revolutions. Democracy has been described as an expedient for 'counting heads to save the trouble of breaking them' – a crude description, but one not to be despised in these days when people are apt to break heads to save the trouble of counting them. On a higher level, democracy has been claimed to contain certain moral ideas by which individuals have rights to be upheld, views to be tolerated, and opportunites of participating in the political process.

There are thus two ways of looking at democracy, neither of which can be ignored. I have tried to set out some of the elements in the charts on pp.118–9. Chart I, I call the Moral View of Democracy, chart II, the Power and Interests View of Democracy. I am well aware that the elements I have listed are incomplete, and also that they belong to different types. I simply give the charts by way of providing a synoptic picture of how I see some of the ingredients in the democratic political process when looked at from two points of view. They are not *alternatives*. It would be wildly unrealistic to give an account of democracy in terms of chart I and not recognise how much, in practice, it runs in terms of chart II. Nor is one chart the mirror image of the other, though certain correspondences and contrasts will be apparent. The moral claim would be that elements set out in chart I can affect what goes on under those set out in chart II, for instance by constraints on acceptable procedures and through pressures stemming from moral convictions and motivations.

Entry A, People are People, appears on both charts, and it might be said that it does so vacuously as it is a mere truism, a tautology. The point is how one passes to B, since on neither chart is B just an implication of A; it incorporates a value judgement. On chart I the transition depends on the conviction that everyone counts by mattering as a person. This value judgement is supported by two factors, x and y. Factor x is not easy to characterise; it is an attitude of mind which I have decided with some hesitation to call 'generosity of spirit'. The other factor, y, is the legal and constitutional recognition that each person has an equal status of citizenship.

On chart II people are seen to count in terms of the part they play in the political process, seen as a struggle of power and interests. Here the practical x factor is the politician's need to get support, and the constitutional y factor is that of universal suffrage. Each citizen plays, minimally, the part of being a voter (note that 'voting' appears on both charts): those concerned with manipulating others politically see them mattering *qua* voters. 'I'd like to help you, son, but you're too young to vote', as Eddie Cochran's song 'Summertime Blues' (c. 1959) has it. Each vote counts because votes are counted numerically. I am here waiving the question of whether each vote counts *equally*; under some electoral systems, such as our 'first past the post', it notoriously does not. I am only saying that politicians are interested in votes, and on a *pure* power and interests view, this is the respect in which ordinary people appear as counting.

'Counts', then, can mean being counted numerically, and it can mean 'matters'. The latter is not only a democratic assertion; it could be held in a number of different kinds of societies, including tribal and feudal ones, provided that everyone has a status which other people respect. The democratic conviction allies this with the assertion of a common adult status of citizenship. Indeed that everyone counts is the fundamental democratic conviction common to rights theories and utilitarian ones. Utilitarians have difficulty in saying how individuals stand in relation to an aggregate social good, but at any rate each has to be taken into account in estimating it – as Bentham said, 'everyone counts for one and no one for more than one'. That everyone counts is a common starting point. The crux is when 'counts' means 'matters'.

Democracy sees people mattering as citizens, a formal institutional status. This would be common ground to members of most political parties. Some, however, take more seriously than others that it has implications in membership of the community. They will protest that some people, in social practice if not in legal status, are second-class citizens. Ralf Dahrendorf in his Tawney Lecture of 1985,[3] has spoken of the growth of what he called the 'underclass', people with no sense of a stake in the country. This, and not the bourgeoisie/workers distinction of Marxism, is now our real class distinction. It is the context in which the word 'alienation' is meaningful.

This leads to the question of equality, a numerical notion applied to people in ways that cannot be measured quantitatively. The difficulties are familiar, and a great deal has been written about them.

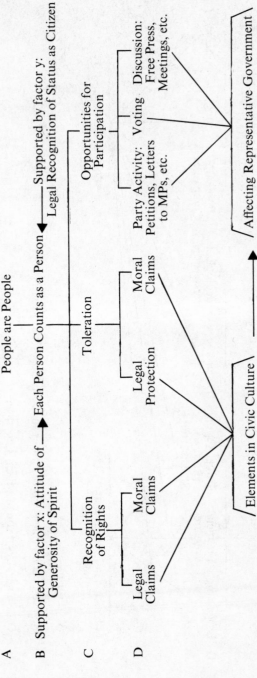

I   MORAL VIEW OF DEMOCRACY

People are People

A

B Supported by factor x: Attitude of ——► Each Person Counts as a Person ——► Supported by factor y:
Generosity of Spirit   Legal Recognition of Status as Citizen

C

D

Recognition of Rights — Toleration — Opportunities for Participation

Legal Claims   Moral Claims   Legal Protection   Moral Claims   Party Activity: Petitions, Letters to MPs, etc.   Voting.   Discussion: Free Press, Meetings, etc.

Elements in Civic Culture ——► Affecting Representative Government

A – Truism

B – Respect in which people matter supported by x and y factors

C – Some ways of giving recognition to B

D – Some ways of implementing C

II   POWER AND INTERESTS VIEW OF DEMOCRACY

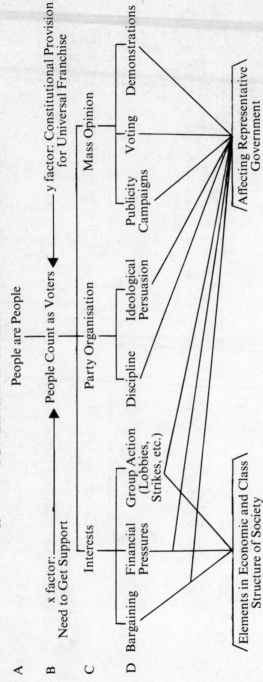

A – Truism

B – Respect in which people matter supported by x and y factors

C – Some ways through which B operates

D – Some ways of implementing C

For its philosophical defenders, equality refers to a belief about the final value of people; for its political defenders, it is a programmatic term with practical implications, especially as regards the distribution of resources.

If there is a sense in which people are said to be equal beyond and in spite of differences in their qualities and capacities, this can take us into a 'spiritual' or 'metaphysical' dimension. Both of these terms are suspect nowadays and there is no satisfactory word for what they are indicating. People were said to be equal as 'children of God', as 'rational beings', or 'by Nature' (a notoriously tricky term). The question is how one testifies in behaviour to an ultimate kind of equality indicated by such phrases.

One answer is that ultimate 'mystical' equality and proximate empirical equality are different in kind, and the former need not have anything to do with the latter. Thus Epictetus, the slave and Stoic philosopher, knew inwardly that he was equal to his master, and was content to leave it like that. But if we are social democrats (whether of the SDP or in a more general sense) we shall not be content to leave it like that. Our conviction that everyone counts is testified to not only by a common status of citizenship, but by a refusal to accept states of affairs where, for instance, unemployment, deficient medical care, lack of, or grossly inadequate, homes, prevent some people from having a stake in the community, and this refusal can focus the idea of equality. Compared with attempts to produce, for instance, equality of incomes (which would need continual adjustments to keep them equal), the insistence that everyone should have sufficient means for taking part in the life of the community can be a realistic and equitable aim.

The quality of life in the community is part of the civic culture which provides the milieu for political activity. By a civic culture I mean one in which there are widespread non-political interests – religious, artistic, commercial, personal – but also a widely shared interest in public affairs. The milieu appears on chart I, but not on chart II, when political activity is represented as going on in a field of conflicting economic and class interests.

That politics goes on in the context of a civic culture with moral overtones is at present being emphasised by the Right. Roger Scruton may be taken as a philosophically articulate representative, both in the columns he writes in *The Times* and in his book *The Meaning of Conservatism*. He sees political obligation as stemming from the loyalty of people living in a civic society based on common traditions, customs, and allegiance to accepted (which here is taken as legitimate) authority. He takes a low view of democracy, which, he says, answers 'neither to the natural nor to the supernatural yearnings of the normal citizen'.[4] Scruton says that it is hard to know whether the populace would miss the vote if they did not have it,[5] a point of view which might surprise those who find themselves disenfranchised. In effect, his enemy is a populist view of participatory democracy. But political democracy does not mean populism; it calls for strong government, yet one in which discussion, not only in parliamentary debates and among interested parties, but also in a host of unofficial circles, can get through to the decision makers. It also calls not for consensus, but for sufficient mainstream opinion to contain the various extremes. This makes for the civic culture of a democracy, and the social morality which sustains a democracy has its roots in the beliefs and practices of this wider setting. In this wider setting people live their lives and pursue their purposes through a host of dealings with each other, where, generally speaking, there is mutual trust and stable expectations about how others are likely to behave.

So the first element in a viable social morality is *custom*. Conservatives see the importance of this element of custom, and indeed if a society coheres largely through customs, it will be conservative with a small c. The word favoured by Conservatives is tradition, which is a grander word. They see tradition as 'concrete' morality, in contrast to the 'abstract' morality of liberalism. This is a view that is likely to appeal more to those who have a secure niche in society than to those who do not: the latter may see the traditions differently and feel 'alienated'.

Customs are a mixed bag. They can be the result of wisdom born of experience; they can be taboos whose reasons, if they had any, have been lost; they can be ways of behaving into which we have, as it were, become programmed. Although, therefore, customs are an inevitable part of social morality, they have to be seen with a critical eye, taking due note of their consequences and resisting the urge to turn them into stereotypes.

Customs are handed on as rules of thumb, and the generalisations behind some of them can be taken as defining how people ought to behave. They then become *principles*. If questioned, the defence is likely to be that principles are rational ways of behaving. Being rational at least means being consistent. A principle applies to cases of the same kind and if we twist or waive it to make exceptions in our own favour we are being inconsistent, or are not being sincere about holding the principle. Note this is a matter of treating like cases alike; it does not say what our principles should be, but only that we should apply them consistently, without fear or favour. We can go beyond mere consistency and take another rational step, that of reciprocity. This calls for detachment, being concerned not only with how a situation affects us, but how it affects other parties: at its best this is an imaginative kind of detachment, a capacity to see how a situation would look if the roles were reversed; for instance if one were at the receiving end of a transaction in which one has been taking a superior position for granted. So 'sauce for the goose is sauce for the gander' morality (consistency in applying principles) can move on to Golden Rule morality (treating others in the kind of way you would like them to treat you). Both bring an element of rationality into morality.

Consistency in the application of principles is not only a matter of formal rationality; it is also a matter of fairness and Rawls speaks of 'justice as fairness'. Justice, however, has other aspects, not least in its connection with law. Rawls is concerned with the distribution of rights, primary goods, and opportunities, and here fairness can be the relevant aspect. Fairness goes with equity rather than with strict equality. It makes for consistency, but this need not be a matter of applying a rule rigorously to all alike, regardless of appropriate differences. In a race where some people have disabilities, it might be fair to give some people a start, which would not be fair in a race where people are presumed fit. The demand for fairness can lie behind the demand for equality of opportunity. The trouble is that in real life the conditions are not set by a few known rules as they are in a game. Some people's life chances will inevitably be more favourable than others. Equality of opportunity could be a way of saying that there should be a career open to talents, and also that everyone should have a fighting chance of living a proper life and given help when the odds are against him. In particular, people need to be able to feel that if they are not in the most advantageous position, they have nevertheless been given a square deal, and that they have not been discriminated against.

It is unfair, for instance, if some take advantage of others, especially when the others are in a weak position, so as to get a better deal for themselves than they could have done if the others had had equal bargaining power. This is exploitation. I should want to go further and say that it is unfair to enjoy advantages at other people's expense, even if we are not deliberately exploiting them. Some of us find ourselves becoming relatively better off through index-linked pensions and increases in the value of our shares. We may not be absolutely better off than we were before because of inflation, but we are increasingly *relatively* better off than people on the lowest incomes, notably the unemployed, and these are the people who suffer most as a result, direct or indirect, of inflation. So the relative affluence of those of us who are more cushioned against inflation can be at the expense of those who are having to bear the brunt of measures taken to curb it. Therefore fairness at least demands that we should not get the kinds of tax concessions which would make the better-off still better off while there are cuts in social benefits. The unfairness of this is not like the unfairness of life. Many things in life are perforce not matters of rational distribution but of good fortune and bad.

This is one reason why we need an infusion of a third element, called on my chart I the x factor, feeding the conviction that people count as persons. It stands for a deeply intuitive side of morality which cannot be prescribed in any set of principles, however rational, nor provided for by conforming to custom. There is a scale here. At one end of the scale this factor is shown in the sacrificial conduct of saints and heroes. But it is also shown all down the scale in all sorts of behaviour in unconvenanted, gracious actions, where people, freely and ungrudgingly, do not just stand on their rights, and where they go beyond what is strictly required or expected of them. Without this element, permeating behaviour in all sorts of ways at every level, the taken-for-granted morality of custom and the deliberate morality of principles can become progressively hardening stereotypes.

It is difficult to find a satisfactory term for this. Fraternity was the third in a trilogy with liberty and equality. But fraternity now sounds male, and I am not prepared each time I use it to add 'and sorority'. Moreover, American student societies have associated these terms with exclusive groups. There are old words which were good ones, like 'grace'. This might be what we want, but it is a word which carries too much theological luggage, especially where it has been thought of as streamlined through authorised channels rather than as something which can transform custom and principle in creative acts. 'Benevolence' was the accepted word among the older British moralists, but this now sounds somewhat avuncular. 'Goodwill' has become too weak; when it was a strong term in Kantian ethics it stood for the disinterested will to do one's duty, which goes with the best side of the impersonal morality of principles. 'Love' has too many connotations, whereas 'tenderness', which has got into SDP parlance, has too few, and so too has 'compassion', which is an overworked word. 'Charity' and 'philanthropy', sound patronising, though the old Latin word *caritas* and the Greek word *philanthropia*, love of mankind, come near to what we want. So too in some contexts does 'mutuality'. I have chosen to call this x factor 'generosity of spirit'.

Generosity of spirit goes beyond mutuality (and certainly beyond the mutuality of tit for tat) in taking initiatives where there may be no response. The word 'generosity' on its own tends to be restricted to contexts where one is in a position to give (though not necessarily money) and so can sometimes be patronising, whereas generosity of spirit can characterise an attitude which one can also have when one is at the receiving end. It cannot replace the morality taken for granted in customs, which, by and large, allows us to trust people; nor can it replace the need for definite rules and principles. But neither can these work in a human way without it.

This is particularly so in administrative behaviour. Here people are dealt with not as individuals but as belonging to kinds, with rules for those falling under the description of each kind. Rules must be general; a rule for an individual would be, in the literal sense, a privilege, a special law for a special person. A rule can be a source of strength, helping the official administering it to act without fear or favour, *sine ira et studio*. It is in the nature of the case impersonal. Hence the common impression of soulless bureaucracy. Indeed, 'soulless' has become an almost inseparable epithet. But if bureaucrats are not soulless, this need not only mean that they have a soul in their off-duty moments. They can also be alert to their 'calling's snare' (Charles Wesley's phrase), which is to escape involvement through sheltering behind the rules of their role. What they can do is constrained by powers under regulations. But there may well be a margin of discretion in applying these, if they are prepared to take the necessary trouble and exercise the necessary ingenuity, and, on occasion, have the necessary courage. Moreover, in spite of the constraints on what can and cannot be done, it is possible to keep alive the awareness that behind the roles of applicants are people who may well be anxious, worried, maybe desperate, while in the roles of the officials are people with secure jobs (though less secure now) and with the prospect of index-linked pensions. There will be the call to know how to listen, and the call for judgement, sometimes for an inspired turning of a blind eye. A wise administrator knows that any set of rules needs loopholes.

Of course, a measure of detachment from one's personal feelings is often necessary in order to do a job. But the avoidance of involvement can give an opportunity for the bully in all of us to use the power of one's position to push people around. The love of power has an emotional force; it feeds one's self-esteem, and can do so at the expense of other people. It will only not do so if it can be met by another deep strain in human nature which feeds generosity of spirit. Initially and naturally this may not be as strong as the desire for power, and it needs training. How does one train it? There are, I suggest, certain conditions:

1 We should believe that generosity of spirit really exists, and may be ready to welcome it, resisting the cynicism, often brittle, clever cynicism, which can always insinuate an ulterior motive. It obviously helps if we have a philosophy which not only allows, but emphasises, generosity of spirit. Christianity does this in most of its forms; so too does liberal humanism where this allows for the heart as well as the head, centring on valuing human beings rather than on opposing religion.

2 We can cultivate interest in people, seeing them with affection and not only enjoying dissecting their characters. This means listening to them.

3 We can cultivate freedom of spirit, more feasible perhaps than directly cultivating generosity of spirit. Freedom of spirit is not absence of feeling; it is detachment from self-involved feelings.

Here the requisite attitude is one the Stoics called *apatheia*. This has had a bad press through being translated as 'apathy'. Apathy suggests insensitivity, if not lack of feeling, for which the Greek word was *anaesthesia*. *Apatheia* is freedom of spirit with regard to emotions such as self-esteem, anxiety, jealousy, vindictiveness – the kinds of emotion which can cloud reason and distort judgement. It gives steadiness – detachment from concern about how one may be affected personally. It can therefore be a state of mind in which clear judgement as well as generosity of spirit may be more possible.

There is no way of escaping the need for judgement. But judgement is not arbitrary; it is a skill, and like other skills it grows through exercise. The people who are likely to do most to develop it will be those who live close (often literally close) to the human problems of our society, and struggle with them without falling into moralistic naivety or amoralistic cynicism. All this calls for critical self-awareness. If it means that democracy is an internal exercise in moral training as well as an external procedure in making public decisions, we must be prepared for this.

SDP members have not sunk their individual judgement in mass views. They can therefore have the freedom of spirit and moral toughness to live with what look like insoluble problems, and to be alert to the possibility of the creative simplification where one sees what should be done. Such judgement is most likely to come when people are living from the roots of social morality in attitudes of will and feeling which feed generosity of spirit, and when they are fighting the attitudes which feed hardness of heart, both in private selfishness and, more insidiously, in blinkered service of a special interest or of what is taken as a public cause.

We are at a parting of the ways: we can get an increasingly divided society and a spread of callousness and violence, or we can get a deepening of the generosity of spirit that feeds civic friendship.

DISCUSSION ON EIGHT

Talking to her paper, Dorothy Emmet warned against attempting to summarise the SDP's political philosophy under any single 'overall' theory, even that of Rawls, to which many social democrats were sympathetically inclined because of the intended fairness of its outcome. Any one theory must be too abstract and general to fit the complexities of a viable social morality. Society could not constitute or reconstitute itself from scratch in accordance with a theory. We needed moral attitudes and convictions developing from the bottom up, not top down. In discussion, nonetheless, it was argued that governments must not be allowed to regard themselves as being above any form of social contract.

The phrase 'generosity of spirit' came in for some criticism on the grounds that people of all parties and of none would subscribe to it and it was therefore not concrete or distinctive enough for our purpose. Dorothy Emmet countered that we should not sound morally exclusive and she was glad it had aroused some interest among certain Labour supporters; without the infusion of something like this democracy couldn't work. Her phrase was also criticised as patronising but received some support in that it was better than 'tenderness' and less patronising than the overworked 'compassion', which had become a codeword for high public spending by bureaucrats laying claim to this quality. 'Generosity of spirit' was embracing enough to activate different principles and motivate different types of people. The important thing was that the structure of society should become permeated by such a concept and bureaucracy humanised and localised. Devolution and the humanisation of institutions were vital, for instance in housing management.

In the search for the right vehicle for that civic culture which Dorothy Emmet wished to see recreated it was suggested that the 'intermediate institutions' of society, such as those envisaged by William Temple (and Keynes) could provide the channels for the development of civic values but that it was especially important that the main business institutions, in particular public corporations, should also recognise their responsibilities and become involved.

In further discussion the need to satisfy people in their

working environment was stressed. But this was not possible if millions were excluded from even the dullest working situation. In this context the emergence of an 'underclass' was again raised. In her paper Dorothy Emmet, following Ralph Dahrendorf, had referred to people with no sense of a stake in the country and had suggested that the old distinction between the bourgeoisie and the workers had been overtaken by this new division between the 'underclass' and the rest of us. If the actual class boundaries were changing as suggested, this was surely of great significance to a party pledged to an 'open, *classless* and more equal society', because it carried the implication that class divisions would be much eroded by the elimination of poverty and the reduction of unemployment. If this was so, it gave added force to the SDP's anti-poverty programme, for which indeed 'generosity of spirit' would be required.

General agreement seemed to emerge from the discussion on Dorothy Emmet's first three 'features' which should characterise the SDP's pursuit of 'democratic politics with moral conviction', namely that this should not be utopian or presuppose a society far removed from our own, for society was not a problem to be solved but a process requiring adequate institutions; that it should avoid a simplistic choice between self-interest and altruism; and that it should recognise the existence of competing groups whose genuine differences liberals always tended to underestimate. On her fourth point, that decisions on public actions should be made generally on utilitarian grounds by people who are not utilitarians 'but know the pull of principle and sentiment', there were some reservations; it smacked slightly of Keynes's élitism fuelled by his 'institutional timidity'; we had agreed we need not be so timid and indeed could not afford to be; certainly there was 'no escape from the need for judgement' but a new framework was now necessary in which that judgement could be exercised.

Armed with the points of general agreement that had emerged from Dorothy Emmet's and previous papers, it seemed we had the foundations of a critical apparatus that could be applied to the political trends with which we were and shall remain in conflict. It was decided, therefore, to take a fresh look at Labour revisionism. Knowing that Danny Finkelstein had recently addressed this subject in a Tawney Society article, we turned to him.

NINE

Revisionists without a Cause

DANNY FINKELSTEIN

'I have not used the word socialism for years,' said Roy Jenkins in an interview with John Mortimer. Though these words were spoken within weeks of his break with his old party, the former Labour Deputy Leader was speaking with complete honesty. In terms of political vocabulary, style and outlook, Roy Jenkins in 1981 was very definitely a colleague rather than a comrade, every inch the biographer of Asquith rather than the political successor to Cripps, a social democrat rather than a democratic socialist.

Most of Roy Jenkins's friends were different. Among those who mourned Gaitskell's death with him, who voted with Heath over Europe with him, even among those who joined the SDP with him, there was a large majority who happily described themselves as democratic socialists. These friends wrote articles for *Socialist Commentary*, dominated the Fabian Society and contributed to the long-standing debates about democratic socialism in the Labour Party. As late as 1980 the Gang of Three – Shirley Williams, David Owen and Bill Rodgers – declared in the *Guardian* that there could be 'no compromise with those who share neither the values nor the philosophy of democratic socialism'.

The formation of the SDP provided the best moment, tactically, for those who joined it to dispense with the 'democratic socialist' label. There has been much criticism of the way in which this was done. David Owen, particularly, has been attacked for removing references to 'democratic socialism' from editions of his 1981 book *Face the Future*.[1] These criticisms notwithstanding, the SDP members were right not to call themselves 'democratic socialists'. By 1981 the views of social democrats had already long ceased to correspond to anything that could sensibly be called socialism.

There were many people – people who had fought against socialist fundamentalism in the Labour Party for the past decade – who did not join the SDP. They chose, instead, to continue to fight for their vision of 'democratic socialism'. They did so in the name of a democratic socialist revisionism developed from the writings of Anthony Crosland and others. They failed to understand that this revisionism could not properly be defined as socialist. They failed to understand, also, that by retaining Crosland's label and by remaining in his party they had rendered themselves incapable of seeing Crosland's faults, as well as his virtues, clearly.

Any distinction between democratic socialism and social democracy is in danger of being merely a semantic squabble. When Lenin talked of social democrats he meant the Marxist SDF. When the IEA in their eccentric tract *An Agenda for Social Democracy*[2] talk of social democrats they apparently mean Norman Tebbit and Margaret Thatcher. When the monetarist atlanticist Peter Jay talks of democratic socialists it is difficult to understand *who* he could mean. Such a word-game is pointless. It is necessary to lay down, firstly, the central elements of democratic socialism before criticising them and then analysing where revisionism stands in relation to such criticisms.

Democratic socialists are those who wish to use what they describe as democratic *means* to achieve socialist *ends*. In the British labour movement they found their chief early voice in the Fabian Society. George Bernard Shaw, H.G. Wells and the infinitely dull Beatrice and Sidney Webb all believed that a collective, commonly owned socialist society could be built gradually through an increasingly benevolent and interventionist state. Beatrice Webb in her diaries summarised the early Fabian vision excellently when she wrote:

> We stake our hopes on the organised working class, served and guided, it is true, by an élite of unassuming experts who could make no claim to superior social status, but content themselves with exercising the power inherent in superior knowledge and larger administrative experience.[3]

The Fabians, with their bureaucratic dreams of a paper-shuffling paradise, were merely the most influential of the democratic socialists. There were others – Christian Socialists, paternalists, the ironically named Owenites and many in the Independent Labour Party. These socialists formed a coalition with the trades unions in the Labour Party. Whatever else they disagreed about, they were all agreed on central principles.

Firstly, they agreed that democratic means could be used, however slow they were, to achieve a socialist Utopia based on full equality and co-operation. This was the most important political difference between Marxists and democratic socialists.

Secondly, they agreed that the socialist society could only be achieved through common ownership of the means of production. This belief was embodied in Clause IV of the Labour Party constitution. A constitutional commitment to common ownership should not be confused with a commitment to more widely distributed ownership or more responsive ownership.[4] Common ownership implied, and was intended to imply, ownership of all the means of production common to all. This form of ownership makes possible a comprehensive national plan – something which was at the heart of the economic debate in the Labour Party in the 1930s.[5]

Thirdly, they agreed that the agents of democratic socialist change were the working class. Labour politicians, such as Ramsay MacDonald, always argued that democratic socialism would benefit all members of society.[6] Against this, however, was the desire of trades unionists to further the particular interests of their members and a class analysis that the democratic socialists partially inherited from Marx. The result has been that democratic socialists have designed their policy proposals in order to win 'the emancipation of the working class'.

When Tony Crosland began to provide a new theory for Labour in the 1950s he contradicted all of these central beliefs. To some of the beliefs his challenge was direct and explicit, but to others it was muted and implicit. This indirectness might have been designed deliberately to protect his position and that of the Gaitskellites. Certainly, he was more sensitive to the mood of the Labour Party than were some of his friends, as his letters to Hugh Gaitskell frequently illustrate.[7] Later in life he was also more inclined than these friends to compromise to this mood as, for example, shown by his actions on Europe in 1972. More likely, however, it was his emotional attachment to the Labour Party that blinded him to the full logic of his own argument. John Vaizey has said, perceptively, that Crosland's attitude to the Labour Party was similar to Evelyn Waugh's attitude to the Catholic Church – having joined it relatively late in life he paid too much attention to its nuns and priests.[8]

Crosland's emotional attachment to Labour constrained his thinking. All his work attempts to square his thinking with socialist and Labour traditions. Similarly, today's democratic socialist revisionists are constantly prevented from more radical thoughts by a desire not to stray too far from traditional democratic socialism.

Taking each of the central elements of democratic socialism in order: democratic socialists are wrong to see political democracy as simply a means to an ultimate end. There will always be differing views, interests and values which will have to be conciliated. For this reason a political system will always be needed and society will always be changing. There is no ultimate end to change. To believe in a perfect society is to believe in 'conservatism deferred' – the possibility of building a society that no one will want to change. Fabians believe that this Utopia is an extremely long way off. Social democrats believe that it does not exist at all. The distinction is important because social democrats believe that political democracy will always be needed and place the imperative that it must work well and fairly at the centre of their thinking. Democratic socialists see democracy simply as a means and demand that it serves socialist ends.

Tony Crosland had obviously read Karl Popper.[9] But he chose to relegate Popper's anti-Utopian arguments to a footnote in *The Future of Socialism*[10] and to continue to talk of means and ends. His revisionist successors have consequently underestimated political reform. They have opposed proportional representation, they have espoused highly centralised government and they have stood in the way of trade union democracy. When members of the SDP began to urge political reforms they were showing clearly the advantage of the freedom which they gained from leaving the Labour Party and losing the democratic socialist label.

On the second element: ever since the work of Berle and Means,[11] and certainly ever since Evan Durbin's book *The Politics of Democratic Socialism*,[12] it has been clear that ownership and control are not the same thing. Increasing social equality and the control of individuals over their own lives does not depend solely on ownership. The experience of nationalisation was not the mass transfer of power to working people but, in many cases, the transfer of power from private managers to public managers. Revisionists like Crosland and Durbin accepted this and argued that there should be an extension of industrial democracy, co-operatives and education for management. However, perhaps they didn't fully understand that rejection of common ownership is rejection of one of the central tenets of democratic socialism. This is why Gaitskell lost his battle to abolish Clause IV. This is why revisionists like Roy Hattersley

champion the mixed economy whilst proposing to strangle private
enterprise. This is why those who do not *ultimately* wish to see
complete public ownership are not democratic socialists. Some revisionists, who understand this, became social democrats. David
Owen's espousal of the 'social market economy' is a reflection of the
fact that social democrats have left the revisionist ambivalence
about profit and private enterprise behind. The revisionists who
stayed in the Labour Party remain simply confused.

Thirdly, the division between ownership and control is reflected in
Britain's class structure. Socialist theory was not developed to cope
with an emerging middle class, with growing working-class
affluence, or with a very different 'underclass'. Both politically (after
the loss of the 1959 general election) and philosophically (ever since
Durbin) the revisionists were well aware that social progress could
not be achieved by class war on behalf of an outdated view of working people. But politically and philosophically the revisionists were
also trapped. Politically they were part of the labour movement
which was dominated by large organised trades unions, and philosophically they had declared themselves as democratic socialists. The
only solution would be to break with both party and label, to establish oneself as an egalitarian who wants to abolish class rather than
win the class war, to fight for social justice rather than vested
interest.

Neil Kinnock has delighted democratic socialist revisionists.
Occasionally he even has the socialist fundamentalists on the retreat.
Their forward march soon begins again because they, at least, know
what they believe. Labour's revisionists, by contrast, are confused
by their label and restricted by their party. This is no condition in
which to fight a battle which is as much ideological as organisational. It is not surprising that they have lost, and lost and lost
again. In the SDP those battles are not necessary, and neither is the
label for which they are fought.

DISCUSSION ON NINE

The discussion on Danny Finkelstein's paper seemed to consolidate further some common ground that had emerged from previous papers, particularly Dorothy Emmet's. The anti-Utopianism of her paper was given fresh backing. If 'democratic socialism' was simply a means to a socialist Utopia, it followed that eventually there would be no need for a political process at all. From this there followed just as naturally the Labour Party's apathy towards reform of a system which at present favoured them electorally and could be discarded when it had served its purpose, like an old husk.

A good deal of attention centred once again on the *incoherence* of Labour's revisionism. The party would perish without socialism, yet was speedily burying whole areas of socialist doctrine, while maintaining Clause IV as an ultimate insurance against accusations of deserting the cause. At the same time it was Clause IV that acted as a real barrier to fresh thinking and inhibited them from offering any coherent response to the New Right. Within the party itself the unions were not interested in socialism – their bread and butter and bargaining power came from capitalism – but they accepted it as a means of access to public subsidy; most nationalised industries had been loss-making since the beginning. There was thus a 'malign ambiguity' at the heart of the movement. Even if Labour were elected, these internal confusions would ensure that it could not survive long in government. The opinion was advanced that a shrinkage of the Labour vote to say 20% over the next ten to fifteen years was almost inevitable and it was even suggested that the Labour rump might become a party of the hard left in favour of proportional representation.

Against this scenario it was argued that the Labour Party could not be written off so easily; there was a lot of heart-searching going on inside the movement about a new decentralism; also it was still able to control the municipal commanding heights. Furthermore, if they were jettisoning their socialist past, didn't this constitute a threat to us?

Perhaps the most important point to emerge from Danny Finkelstein's paper was the clear distinction drawn by him between 'democratic socialism' and social democracy, which believed unequivocally in the continuing need for a political process with reformed institutions; we too had a vision but ours was one of a constantly renewable idea with a political vehicle adequate to accommodate differing views. It was suggested from one quarter that the Finkelstein paper did not include enough legislative thought. In opposition to this criticism it was pointed out that we believed in a process which we would not necessarily dominate in terms of legislation. The argument about values versus legislation was important if a coalitition was in prospect; in this eventuality we should be expected to bring certain values to bear on the governmental process – which was different from the 100% implementation of a legislative programme. It was further suggested that parliament was widely seen as 'yah-boo' and was unpopular; therefore our reforms of government should be up front.

When the problem of the SDP's identity was raised and concern expressed that the Thatcher government had already taken over some of our policies, the contrary view was put that we should be flattered that we were the source of good ideas for other parties. From another quarter the idea of a blurred identity was roundly rejected: did not 'open, classless and more equal' say it all? Openness committed us to government reform, classlessness to wider educational possibilities and greater equality to redistribution. Also, our belief in the continuing importance of the public services made us very distinct from the Tories.

The extent of our commitment to the satisfaction of the consumer of public services was further discussed. A complaint was made that David Owen was very 'macho' on profit; did he have to take it so far? He reiterated the profit motive till it hurt. Here it was pointed out that the Labour Party was so against profit that it was inevitably drawn towards central government planning. But the most important task over the next decade was to reverse our industrial decline, which would not be achieved by the dead hand of the planner. In response to the concern that we were in danger of delivering a charter for property developers, it was emphatically reasserted that we were not in favour of a *laissez-faire* market economy but of a social market economy: capitalism and socialism both belonged to the nineteenth century and were both obsolescent; the old -ism parties were on the wrong track. However, there was now a more recent -ism, Thatcherism, which we could not ignore. Nick Bosanquet offered to give us a paper drawing on his book *After the New Right*.

TEN

Challenging the New Right

NICK BOSANQUET

The New Right is not monolithic, with a single view of the world. But for its main contributors some themes recur:

The operation of the economic market provides the main force that matters for higher growth.

Society, and the economy within it, have an inherent tendency towards order and progress. Disturbance and regress arise through the actions of government.

Capitalism has vastly improved living standards and prospects, in the short and long run. Capitalism depends on enterprise. The role of the entrepreneur is critical.

Inequality is the inevitable and tolerable result of social freedom and personal initiative.

Growth will eliminate poverty in absolute terms which are the only terms which matter.

There are many qualifications, differences between thinkers and inconsistencies within particular writers' work.[1] Frequently there is a tension between economic liberalism and social authority. Can a world in which almost all state restrictions on economic activity have been removed also be one in which the state intervenes to maintain traditional social values?

On each of these main propositions social democratic and social liberal thought offers a reasoned alternative. The aim of this chapter is to spell these out.

The Role of the Market

The central contention especially of what could be called the political or Thatcherite Right is that family drive and initiative in markets will bring about the best results not just for the family, but for the economy. The market is the main means through which the family achieves its ends. There are other current dimensions to family choice and activity but the New Right argues that these dimensions are either of private significance or ought to be diminished because they represent a past heritage of collectivism. These other dimensions are:

The unpaid work done by household members in the care of children or other dependents – work which may affect their ability to earn income in the labour market.

The network of neighbourhood and community associations which contribute to leisure, family support, and through which people develop their interests and skills.

The rights of family members as citizens in political choice, both through the ballot box and through the political process.

The interests of family members as consumers of public services as well as of goods and services in private markets.

The position of the New Right on each of these dimensions needs spelling out. Within households, the preference of the New Right is for the traditional division of labour assisted by traditional moral precepts. The neighbourhood dimension is accepted as having some importance, but is secondary to the market: there is little recognition of a possible conflict between community and neighbour interests and the market. If people are left free to choose in markets they will also be in the most advantageous position to develop community and neighbourhood activities as well.

The New Right's view of the political system is that the choices made through it should be kept to a minimum. The political system is a far less successful method of making decisions than the market. Friedman made the early case and much of Hayek's later work is the extended indictment of the political process. There is a much less coherent or united view on this than on the role of the market: but the following strands of analysis appear. Voters are ill-informed and it is rational to expect them to remain ill-informed; the political process will be dominated by powerful interests – usually producer interests which have the most incentive to do so. Of these producer interests public sector unions will be by far the greatest obstacles to the efficient operation of the market. The political process will be best served by the election of strong governments of the Right which will guard the ramparts of the market in the years between elections.

The right to vote is largely an unfortunate historical accident: in any sane community it will become increasingly redundant as people gain their goals through market processes. In practice political authority may become a despotism tempered by middle-class pressure groups.

The political process awaits a strong government to roll back the collectivism of the past. In the longer term, politics will wither away. Political conflict is a tainted legacy from the collectivism of the past, and will not be a major feature of a society in which the free market has its proper place. In essence the rights of family members as voters are best used sparingly to elect strong governments. In between elections the need for political expression will not arise in a society in which the market is allowed to function efficiently.

The interests of family members as consumers of public services are an illusion, a state of mind also conditioned by a collectivist past. The real interest of family members is to see these public services put under the re-animating disciplines of the market. Once the market has been given its head public services as known in the past will wither away. Men and women will find their true selves beneath the false self left by the collectivist past.

Against this unitary view of the market as the prime and sole way in which the household can achieve its goals in the long run, the social democratic approach stresses that pluralism, diversity and conflict are permanent and inherent in the way that the household relates to the outside world. The well-being of individuals and households has to be seen in terms of a number of *different* dimensions. People buy goods and services in markets and they sell their own labour time; but they are also family members; they have ties to neighbourhood and local communities. They are citizens exercising public choice through representative democracy; they are consumers of public services. This pluralism is not a hangover from a collectivist past but represents the essential diversity of life outside the private sphere. Each of these dimensions represents permanent ways in which people will relate to their environments. Above all there is an inevitable tension and likely conflict between market processes and these other dimensions.

The household may have dependent children – or disabled or elderly members. Fulfilling commitments here will often involve sacrifice of market opportunity in terms of consumption, work and career development. There may be some who are capable of advancing all their interests at the same speed; but households are not working for the most part just to market incentives, in the narrow sense. There are other aims in life than those of raising real income as rapidly as possible; in fact pursuit of these goals may make it very difficult even to maintain current levels of real income. Markets can advance human values – but they are not the only way of doing so and they may conflict with other ways of doing so. Differences in dependency and the conflict between the interest of family members in the market and their responsibilities for dependents are an inherent feature of life.

The dimension of neighbourhood and community is not a simple one. It stretches from very local relationships to a few neighbours through voluntary associations over a wider area which might be local, regional or even national. The relationships and experiences here may influence developments in markets; but this sphere provides a whole area of life which is of vital importance and which is distinct from the relationships set in markets. This sphere of relationships also contributes directly to the attitudes which make it possible for markets to operate. The ability to act constructively and to maintain co-operation in a market demands qualities and attitudes produced outside the market.

The exercise of political rights is not a hangover from a collectivist past but the main means through which households redress the imbalance of power between themselves and producer groups in society. There are many conflicts of interest which arise in an urban environment where one man's property rights inevitably affect others'. These conflicts cannot be resolved just by electing a strong majoritarian government every four or five years. They require a political system in which political choices can be made in a responsible way and after both the strong and the weak have had a full chance to put their point of view. Social democrats want to spell out conditions for an effective representative democracy. These conditions will change over time as social circumstances and access to information change; but the exercise of political rights through protest, advocacy or advancement of interest will remain a major theme in society. The New Right has certainly identified one major problem – which is that under the current system of political democracy undue weight is often given to the interests of producer groups. But this does not mean that there will not always be insistent pressures towards a powerful and effective representative democracy.

People are also consumers of public services. There may well be a case for moving away from public sector monopoly: but the real interests of people in current standards of goods and services are still there. There may be yearnings for a better system – but this will be a long time in coming. The New Right may wish that people were *not* consumers of public services and that the public services did not exist: but at present they do and the interest of the current groups of consumers should be given much greater weight; not least in the case of education where each child only has one childhood and one experience, and cannot decide to switch to an alternative product. In its wish to reduce the span of public services, the New Right may well end up with a collectivism of the Right by which the public monopoly remains but the supply of services is reduced.

Society's Inherent Order

The New Right is optimistic. *Laissez-faire* is only workable in a world in which private initiative contributes to general order. 'What institution of government could tend so much to promote the happiness of mankind as the general prevalence of wisdom and virtue? All government is but an imperfect remedy for these deficiencies.'[2] Coercion arises above all from the effects of big government.

Social democrats see private coercion as a major force in society. Coercion – in the sense of a restriction of the opportunities and choices open to certain citizens for the private interest of other citizens – could arise from the activities of professions or producer groups. In some societies the influence of clans, dynasties and extended families is great and even in Britain it can be quite important. Such groups have strong incentives to secure their positions locally and nationally. Some of them will have advantages not just of income and security but of preferential access to debate and the power to deny unpopular opinions a hearing. There is no strong interest in maintaining a free society or even the conditions for free markets. In fact particular interests usually run the other way, towards trying to undermine a free society and the operation of free markets. The conditions even for economic competition do not establish themselves through the free decisions of private agents who usually have an interest in repressing competition.

Economic vested interests are not the only form of private power or even the one with the most serious possible impact on freedom. Vested interests will show great energy in pursuit of their aims but their aims may well be limited. People driven by strong beliefs or prejudices (to others) do not have limited aims. There is no boundary at which inertia begins to set in. The exercise of private power may feed on itself and become a tyranny. The New Right shows concern about the private power exercised by trades unions but almost nothing about the activities of cultural and religious groups. People driven by strong prejudices can show even greater energy and will to dominate as their hold on society grows. The open society with free competition and tolerance lives under threat from religious and cultural obsessions.

For social democracy, there is a presumption that the strong in society will try to tilt the balance against the weak. The market in fact contributes to this by raising the income and ability to act of some. There are limits to the extent that market power should override rights in other spheres. There is the possibility of safeguards for the rights of minorities through the political and legal process. The rule of law implies a developed constitutionalism and a framework of rights. It implies that the freedom of action of the strong is limited. Constitutionalism means in Hume's phrase that the 'observance of justice' is made 'the immediate interest of some particular person.'[3] These issues have become even more important in the last two decades when the deferential and hierarchical society of the past has gone beyond recall. Instead there is a society in which expectations are higher, comparisons easier and inequality more resented. It is a society of greater ethnic and ideological diversity in which discrimination is at one and the same time less acceptable and more entrenched. It is a society in which there will be threats to tolerance and even to public order, yet one in which repression is likely to be fitful, inconsistent and ultimately unsuccessful. It is a society which will need to draw on any reserves of toleration and of imagination over the next few decades and in which the political and constitutional system needs reform to take account of many new problems. This system was developed for the earlier era of deference and hierarchy and is under increasing strain where there are strong and insistent demands for due process and for representation; where there are greater differences of ideology and belief; and where there are new balances to be struck between majorities and more diverse and more insistent minorities. The routine of majority rule and of conventional opinion is not enough to maintain the minimum of consent in civil society. It is also difficult to fit to the greater creati-

vity and adaptability required by individuals and communities in a
rapidly changing economy. Against the broad optimism of *laissez-faire*, social democratic thought presents the need for development
of a new constitutionalism and a framework for the exercise of
public and private power in a much more diverse society.

The Benevolence of Capitalism

The New Right argues that capitalism has vastly improved living
standards in the long term and certainly this is true over a period of
twenty years or more. In the long term capitalism produces benign
results, as economic growth works to cheapen consumption. Goods
and services which were luxuries become much more accessible. A
household income at 80% of the average buys much more in real
terms in 1985 than it did in 1959. In the long run – so long as the
social security system operates to redistribute them – most people do
get some share in the returns to economic growth.

In the short term economic growth has a different face and one
ignored by the New Right. It appears as economic change with large
changes in income, employment chances and living standards affecting individuals and communities. There are some greater inequalities between age groups. Younger workers will be more highly
qualified, more mobile to take advantage of new opportunities and
more attractive for employers' investment. The fifty-year-old engineering worker faced with redundancy in Newcastle or Bolton is
unlikely to be overwhelmed by offers from employers in sunrise
industries eager to develop his productivity. He will be lucky to find
another job as a taxi-driver or a supermarket storeman. Nor is he
likely to have a large occupational pension to look forward to. Even
if he was in a scheme at all in his old firm, the pension will be worth
little without the last fifteen years of contributions.

Clearly economic change has been particularly rapid since 1979.
The changes in employment since then have been as great as those
which took place in the preceding two decades. The main losers in
these years have been older manual workers ejected from manufacturing. A capitalist economy carries the freedom to introduce new
products and processes which undercut the livelihood of some
people. The New Right's answer to this would seem to be in terms of
private foresight before the event and active mobility after it.
However, the effects of economic change are ones against which it is
not possible to insure and which are totally unpredictable. A young

worker joining the steel industry in Consett, County Durham in 1960 may have thought that he had a job for life. Now the grass is growing over the old plant site. Mobility is only a partial answer. After a certain age people will be more and more unwilling to move and may find it increasingly difficult to invest in new skills. However much the supply price may fall, employers will not be tempted to invest heavily in the specific training of middle-aged workers when they can recruit younger ones. The process of economic change takes place across the generations.

Economic change also increases the differences between communities. A town can become the prisoner of its own past. There used to be some recognition of this in economic thinking through the concept of the external effect. Firms became concentrated in a particular area and this concentration created effects external to the firm which lowered its internal costs. Some of these effects could arise from access to common services or to specialised skill in the labour market. The evidence on regional and local development in Britain shows that such external effects are part of a far wider set of changes by which certain areas become more attractive to new industries. An area may be lucky in having some activities which show sudden growth or it may turn out to have a favourable location for a new industry. Once the momentum is there for local incomes and employment it becomes easier for people to start new firms in response to local markets. There will be more chances for promotion and for acquiring skills on the job. The area will begin to attract migration from outside. Children will grow up in more prosperous homes with greater incentives to get qualifications. Local housing values rise and the local environment improves. Decisions on public expenditure based on changes in population on traffic flows and on rate of return calculations will favour such areas.

Other communities face a winding road towards decline. This may begin from a demand shock which brings about the closure of an important local employer. Local employment and output declines and it becomes less attractive to start new businesses. Workers have less opportunity or incentive to develop skills and qualifications. Young people migrate out and any potential new employers begin to see the area as presenting recruitment problems for qualified manpower. There is an interaction between the decisions of households and those of firms in such an area, which means that declining output and employment react on household aspirations and the change there makes it even more difficult to attract new employers. The local housing market follows unemployment into decline. In local politics the role of the local public sector grows and there may be an increase in bitterness which quickens the flight by employers. The operation of markets leads to cumulative changes which create fundamental differences in the prospects of local communities.

Social democracy accepts that there will be a continuing conflict between the goal of economic growth in the long term and its means of economic change in the short term. 'We' may all gain from economic growth – but 'we' certainly do not all gain from the process by which economic growth takes place. In practice, economic change will often lead to economic and human loss through the wasted abilities of the losers and political conflict as they fight back through the only channels open to them, which are the political ones.

The aim is a set of policies which will encourage adaptation to economic change. Such adjustment is not merely the capital adjustment for which the usual incentives are relevant in terms of profitability. Adjustment is also required on the labour side. Some argue as if adjustment to economic change was best assisted by great insecurity and uncertainty, but such conditions would seem more likely to encourage a sense of desperation, a fight to the finish which will greatly increase political tensions. The New Right's emphasis on huge prizes for winners and losses for the rest will heighten and intensify the very process of self-destructive politicisation which it abhors. For social democrats, economic change will not be left to take its own course. There is a constant search for policies in compensation, for developing potential and for winning consent for the process of change and growth. The Keynes of the *Yellow Book* has much more to offer here than the Keynes of the *General Theory*.

Social democrats also disagree profoundly with the New Right's interpretation of the role of the entrepreneur. Entrepeneurial drive plays a vital role but it uses the material of the society and the economy around it. The entrepreneur needs a legal, social and economic environment. The contributions of many people at many points are required to back the entrepreneur's vision. Most obviously the entrepreneur depends on the loyalty and sense of initiative of his workforce in building his business. Without co-operation entrepreneurialism may lead simply to the growth of a plutocracy rather than of a successful mixed economy.

The 'Inevitability' of Inequality

The focus of the New Right is on *equality* and on its costs. If inequalities increase this simply reflects market outcomes and no sensible person will worry about them. The arguments have been best put by the late Lord Robbins. The pursuit of equality is usually used to blur four quite distinct alternatives. There is equality before the law; equality of opportunity; equality of reward and equality of property.[4] Equality before the law presents no difficulty – this is perfectly acceptable. Equality of opportunity is a reasonable aspiration but will never be realised in practice because of differences in home background. It is equality of reward which is wholly objectionable. There is a case for spending to relieve poverty in an absolute sense – but beyond this there is no case for any levy on personal income. According to Lord Robbins: 'The inequality of reward which the market system engenders does not seem to me something which persons of good sense should worry about over much.' There is also much writing on the evil effects of progressive taxation and on the importance of people being able to take risks in order to win large fortunes.

The philosophy of social democracy accepts that there is room for large rewards to economic initiative – but there are types of inequality other than those which arise from such initiative. Inequality comes in several brands and the most common is that of social deprivation which reduces people's ability to contribute to society. Through inequality in access to the labour market, through rising unemployment and through the harmful effects of social segregation brought on by the misguided collectivism of the housing past, many people can become trapped in poor conditions, low expectations and even worse prospects. Such inequality is not inevitable, tolerable or socially functional. It is a disaster for individuals and a tragic loss of potential for society. Such deprivation is not accidental or temporary but a major part of the current social state – in fact many of the dynamics of the policy of the Right over the past seven years have made the problem of deprivation much worse.

Social democrats share the sense of outrage at the waste of deprivation with many socialists. Where they part company from socialists is in their willingness to look at all means in terms of public and private action to give the suppressed, ignored and deprived a chance to take charge of their own destinies. For example, a policy for helping people in the inner cities must involve a really sustained effort to attract new private capital – on this, all agree. Social democrats go beyond this in being prepared to face all the difficult problems raised by a certain type of militant trade unionism in making the inner cities unattractive to such capital. For socialists the white horse of social concern is harnessed to the black horse of the old public sector. Some, as in Sheffield and elsewhere, may be struggling to reconcile the socialist faith with the requirements of adaptation and change – but it has been a painfully slow and difficult process. Public initiative certainly has a role – but an expanding role only once the link is broken between public initiative and public monopoly. The deprived and the excluded require above all power and choice and these can be sought effectively only through new combinations of public and private initiative.

The New Right and Poverty

The New Right would confine the definition of poverty to the absolute sense of the term – the minimum required for physical subsistence. This implies that society has an interest in maintaining the lives of its members on a purely physiological or animal basis but does not care about whether people's ability to function mentally and socially is maintained. A different approach would stress that life is not just about physiological existence: it is also about relationships, activity and dignity. The definition of poverty in absolute terms is hardly defensible in humanistic terms: it may also be a poor business proposition. Poverty and unemployment lead to dependence. If people have to struggle to maintain even the barest pretence of a normal existence in society their chances of getting a job will be reduced. A definition in absolute terms implies that society should be indifferent to future potential for independence. The relative definition sets standards in terms of those which are needed to maintain self-respect in a particular society at a particular time. The New Right's rejection of the relative definition involves a view of human life which is both short-sighted and profoundly dispiriting.

The absolute definition is of course highly convenient in taking attention away from the growing number of people who are in poverty by the conventional definition – tainted with relativism – of the supplementary benefit scale rate. The much decried social secur-

ity system has suceeded in reducing poverty among elderly people;
but the effects of higher unemployment have greatly increased
poverty among disabled people and among families with the head in
full-time work so that the total number of people dependent on supplementary benefit or with incomes below the supplementary benefit
scale rates was eight million in 1985, or 18% of the population. The
poor, by the normal and not very generous definition, are not a tiny
and disappearing minority: such figures dictate the conditions of
daily living for millions of people. In an economy where 36% of
households in 1985 had no income from the labour market and little
income from any other sources, the issues of poverty and redistribution are seen very differently by social democrats than from the
perspective of the New Right. The philosophy of social democracy
and social liberalism is prepared to make the case for progressive
taxation and developed public services to ensure that people can
share in the gains of economic growth. They accept too that there
are limits to this redistribution and that it could go so far as to
threaten incentive and the growth process itself: but for this, practical calculations need to be made as the economy and society change.
At present the balance has swung too far away from equality and
redistribution through incentive, to plutocracy.

Conclusions

The main propositions of social democracy to contrast with those of
the New Right can be summed up as follows:

> The operation of the economic market is modified by other
> important relationships. People have family obligations: they
> have ties to neighbourhoods and to local communities: they are
> voters and users of public services. Progress comes from getting a
> balance between the varied and often conflicting priorities.

> Society has no automatic tendency to progress if left alone by
> government. There are threats from private coercion as well as
> from the abuse of public power and these will require the
> development of a genuine constitutionalism.

> Capitalism improves living standards through economic growth
> in the long run – but in the short run the process of economic
> change sets up new inequalities. The rise in productivity of some
> people may drag everyone up in the long run but in the short

there are great costs to those that are rejected. These require programmes for compensation and adaptation.

Entrepreneurs operate within a social context. The contributions of many people at many points are required to back the entrepreneur's vision; these all have human and economic significance. Entrepreneurialism can lead simply to the resurgence of plutocracy.

Inequality comes in several brands. Social democrats are most concerned about chronic social deprivation which makes it impossible for people to contribute to or participate in the 'open' or 'great' society.

Poverty has to be defined in terms of prevailing standards and by such standards it is showing an increase which represents hardship and an immense loss of potential.

Nick Bosanquet wound up his talk by saying that the response of the New Right to the growing dependency on the state that went with economic decline was to declare that all public sector activity was bad *per se*. But there was also a collectivism of the Right, and Friedman's belief that the interests of the Right were best served by the withdrawal of the state from the economic arena was curiously paralleled by the belief of socialism that the state was central to its purpose. What we should be concentrating on was how to create a 'civil society' to which many different groups and backgrounds could contribute. The SDP was not about equality but about redefining the conditions of freedom.

Nick Bosanquet was then asked which was more important to the New Right – economic theory or gut feeling? He thought mainly gut feeling but the sense that they had the intellectual upper hand was important to them too; because of the discredit into which socialism had fallen and the incoherence of Labour (brought out by Danny Finkelstein), they felt there was no serious force that could oppose them. Social liberalism had been coming along nicely at the time of the *Yellow Book* but when the Labour Party took over as the alternative party in the state, the Liberals retreated into the 'small is beautiful' corner of the political argument. Some of the New Right were saying to us that we should be with them in five years. We should be saying to them that our task was the revival of social liberalism after the long socialist interlude.

Worry was then expressed about how you controlled private economic power without erecting over it a public power which was even more unaccountable; there was no such thing as a pure private monopoly, but pure public monopolies, indeed there were. Nick Bosanquet agreed that there had to be an incredibly good reason for a public monopoly. Crosland had come to the same conclusion in supporting housing associations. How to get a feeling for the public good without creating public monopolies – that was the essential question.

Another concern sprang from liberalism's association with, indeed fundamental commitment to, choice; we now had large numbers who were so (relatively) poor that they could not shop around. At what level did consumer choice begin? Some people were trapped in an 'underclass', and it was asked whether welfare did not itself perpetuate this new phenomenon. If the basics continued to be provided for humanitarian reasons, how did you ever break out of the cycle of dependency? When people were excluded from the labour market, Nick Bosanquet replied, they were getting the worst slice of whatever was going: bad clothing, bad housing, bad health and so on were self-perpetuating. It was a fact seldom appreciated that 36% of households had no income from the labour market. When asked what this percentage would be at full employment, the answer was 25%; even so the 11% difference represented a significant wastage of human resources and was a cause of grave social malaise. When markets moved and left people high and dry, action had to be taken.

The discussion moved to reform of the labour market and to tax reform. We had virtually no capital taxation in the UK and very heavy labour taxation; the incentives were all to capital; manufacturing industry now produced the same output with 25% fewer workers. But disincentives to capital were not desirable either, it was argued; if the level of investment was increased you could increase productivity without losing jobs. From another quarter it was urged that macro-economic policy had to go hand-in-hand with labour market reform. For a long time it had been assumed that only the macro-level of government policy counted. The proper SDP position was to pay attention to both. For example, a switch to expenditure taxation would provide a better income for the poor in work. We should steal the Tories' clothing for a change and raise incentives. If the tenant on the Broadwater estate could keep more, he would go out and get work.

On the question of the invisible line between centre-right and centre-left, redistribution emerged as the acid test. Markets only decided production. The moral issues (as Meade had pointed out) attached to distribution. There was enough surplus invested in BMWs to fund the redundant workers in Glasgow. The New Right would condemn any such redistribution as coercion, but both rights-based and utilitarian arguments pointed to some redistributive mix. The difficulty, whether from a Rawlsian or utilitarian standpoint, was to get that mix right in order not to destroy wealth creation. The trouble with some Tories was that they had got the balance wrong, because they didn't *mind* about poverty, which occurred only because people were feckless or irresponsible;

they didn't *mind* about the mentally ill; they didn't really *mind* about drug addiction – New Right theorists would simply decriminalise heroin in order to cut street prices on a straight-forward 'choice' argument without counting the human cost.

A note of warning was uttered that most of our attention had been concentrated on the casualties of the system. Nick Bosanquet was again pressed to say how we could become a more successful economy while maintaining a high level of public services. His answer was that a 'civil society' with proper public services and wider choices would produce a better economic record in the long run. After all, the Tories had little to write home about on this score; though they had enriched some they had done little for the economy as a whole and had certainly not begun to reverse our relative economic decline. Ultimately, their disqualification was that they were tied to vested interests; they were simply about plutocracy and private power.

Our task, he concluded, was to attack New Right assumptions on the lines he had suggested. The economic market was the engine of growth but that did not mean the public sector belonged to the Prince of Darkness; there were threats from private coercion as well as from the abuse of public power. Capitalism improved living standards in the long run but there were great short-term costs to certain groups from economic change; the SDP was concerned with *change* as much as *growth*. The role of the entrepreneur was indeed critical but he depended on many inputs and could not operate outside the social context. Some inequality was inevitable and natural but much of it was unnecessary and unacceptable; we would not accept chronic social deprivation which marginalised millions. Poverty was on the increase and it was absurd to measure it by absolute rather than relative standards. The New Right's model of the polity allowed for none of these things. Ours did; that was the great difference between us.

CONCLUSION

I undertook in the introduction not to attempt to impose a spurious harmony on these essays. And in the brief passages on the discussions I think I have indicated that there are differences of approach and in one or two cases, of substance. Nonetheless, I believe I shall be able to show that these are perfectly healthy differences which can be accommodated within the framework of social democracy; I also believe they are much outweighed by the very high level of agreement that emerged on the central issues of state power and economic power.

British social democracy is largely about the revival of liberalism. This is not an argument for or against an eventual merger of the Social Democratic Party with the Liberal Party. It is simply a statement of fact. There were, as David Marquand and Robert Skidelsky reminded us, two previous Liberal revivals, the first being that of the 'new' Liberalism associated with L.T. Hobhouse's book *Liberalism* (1911), whose close affinity with socialism received a serious setback with the Russian Revolution of 1917. The second revival, associated in this country with the names of Keynes and Beveridge, had a much more managerial emphasis and basically proceeded by stealth. By this time the Liberal Party had been superseded by the Labour Party as the second party in the state and Labour became the only possible vehicle for the plans of liberal intellectuals. The third liberal revival, the present one, was set in motion by the defection of senior Labour politicians at serious odds with the doctrinaire socialism and insular chauvinism which that party had developed; this was immediately followed by the formation of a new party, 60% of whose adherents had no previous connection with any political party whatever.

Our group at once recognised the debt of the new movement to continental social democracy and, in the first essay in this book, Roger Morgan traced the links and identified the similarities and the differences between British social democracy and the main continental parties broadly within the social democratic tradition. But the major influences on our brand of social democracy are clearly to be found within the British progressive tradition. In his essay David Marquand taught us to face up to the difficulties confronting the 'middle way' in British politics. In Britain consensus had always fallen apart on the apparently irremediable antagonism between egalitarianism and efficiency. But why was this so when other democracies had pursued the middle way with comparative success? The answer appeared to lie in the immutable Westminster model of parliament. This remained sacrosanct to Liberals of the first and second revivals and remains so to Conservatives and Labour revisionists to this day. Yet one of the great failings of this model is that it is prevented by its egocentricity from sharing power, either outwards with supranational bodies or downwards with local authorities. It is incapable of adaptation. Its reluctance to change stems from the settlement of 1689, which made parliament supreme. Ever since, the Crown-in-Parliament has been the embodiment of the British state. But this 'state' can and now usually does become the property of a single political party with a minority of votes in the country, exclusively pursuing its own interests. It is at this point that one begins to suspect that Britain's economic ills have basically political causes and it is, I think, a special insight of British social democracy that constitutional reform is a precondition of economic revival.

This analysis was carried further by Robert Skidelsky in his essay on Keynes. None of the progressive reformist parties of the inter-war or the post-war years has had any adequate theory of the state – largely no doubt because of the discredit into which the idea of a strong state had been thrown by communism and fascism. Keynes's 'institutional timidity' sprang partly from this and partly from his respect for Burke's constitutional conservatism. His 'somewhat comprehensive socialisation of investment' was founded on the belief that existing institutions – the Bank of England, the universities, the civil service and the large corporations whether in the public or private sector – would, by some peculiar internal metamorphosis, be increasingly managed in the public interest, making nationalisation superfluous, indeed irrelevant. Yet subsequent experience has not been happy. The corporatism of the fifties and sixties (which followed logically from this view) failed ultimately, because it had been stitched up behind closed doors in smoke-filled rooms and not openly negotiated in the forum of parliament; in the seventies it had to be abandoned.

What then are we left with? We are confronted starkly with the unpalatable truth that the tie-beam of our unwritten constitution – the Crown-in-Parliament – is at the mercy of 'a congeries of competing politicians', one faction of which after each election seizes the power of the Prince deposited in parliament in order to promote the interests of its own supporters during its tenure of office (which could, incidentally, without much difficulty, be extended indefinitely by a repeal of the Parliament Acts which are not and cannot be entrenched). At the end of his essay Robert Skidelsky asks the chilling question: 'Is the Prince inevitably and irretrievably tainted by corruption? Or is he our main safeguard against it?' As things stand, the answer has to be that he is tainted and he is not our safeguard. Mediaeval princes had at least to share power with their vassals; and when a vassal abused his portion of power the Prince would often step in to protect his subjects. In such cases he was indeed their safeguard. No such checks and balances exist in the British constitution.

Small wonder, then, that social democrats attach great importance to the reform of our institutions. Yet, when we come into this area we immediately find ourselves up against the weight and inertia of the British empirical tradition, which was strongly influenced by Benthamite utilitarianism. Because it is difficult to introduce reforms against the grain, we devoted some time to this tradition. Though Smith and Hume used the term 'utility', they were not in the modern sense utilitarians, because eighteenth-century harmony demanded a balance between 'self-love' and 'benevolence'. George Goyder demonstrated that *The Wealth of Nations* could not be properly read in isolation; one had also to take into account *The Theory of Moral Sentiments*. But benevolence dropped out with Bentham (though it later crept back in with Sidgwick). In the hands of J.S. Mill the thrust of utilitarianism was altered towards liberty through self-government and Alan Ryan expressed the view that 'utilitarian ways of thinking which are commonly thought to favour a pretty brutal, pro-capitalist and anti-egalitarian political philosophy may perfectly naturally lead to better things . . .' It is of course true that utilitarianism working through markets, does have an anti-hierarchical and egalitarian component.

Here, however, perhaps the widest rift developed in our group. Utilitarianism was roundly condemned by Inigo Bing and Kevin Carey on the grounds that it did not recognise any fundamental natural rights. Some degree of liberty might be a by-product of Benthamism; it certainly was not its aim. They argued that we now required a contractual model and advanced the one invented by the American philosopher, John Rawls, in *A Theory of Justice*, in con-

junction with the emphasis on rights developed by Ronald Dworkin.
It is indeed true that the British citizen has never had a set of rights
guaranteed by a written constitution; after 1689, power rested
increasingly and then fully with parliament which is subject to no
higher law. It was possibly distaste for the American and revulsion
from the French Revolutions that led us to distrust 'pieces of paper'
and put our faith in such hallowed but unguaranteed conventions as
'free speech' and 'freedom of the press'. But the fact remains that
rights are more easily introduced where the framework or basic
structure already exists and there can be no doubt that Rawls is
writing very much from within the American tradition with its
supreme court and its separation of powers. Owing to our constitutional development along quite different lines, the immediate leap
to a bill of rights would be extremely difficult. A society cannot
reconstitute itself from scratch except by revolution – or by the
natural demise of a previous régime as was recently the case in
Spain. But we are not in that situation. Thus, combining the rights
movement with the British empirical tradition, by far the best way
forward would seem to be the incorporation of the European
Convention of Human Rights into domestic law, buttressed by a
Ministry of Justice – which some jurists regard as an essential first
step. These are the prerequisites of a 'lean set of rights' to which
utilitarians can subscribe on instrumental grounds, though contrac-
tualists and rights-theorists will eventually want to go further. But
British social democrats are not revolutionaries and, to gain acceptance in Britain, the entrenchment of citizens' rights will have to be
an evolutionary process.

The rift between utilitarians with their consequentialism and the
champions of a written contract between the citizen and the state
was put in perspective, it seems to me, by Dorothy Emmet's paper.
She warns against placing absolute faith in abstract models and
shows that rights-based theories and utilitarianism do have one very
important thing in common, namely that 'everyone counts for one
and no one for more than one'. It is true that 'counts' in Benthamite
terms can only be interpreted numerically, while rights-theorists will
want to endow that word with the additional weight of 'matters'.
But it is a significant area of common ground and it brings both
sides of the argument together in a commitment to representative
government – which we certainly do not enjoy in this country today.

In her essay, but not in her essay alone, great importance is also attached to the *process* of democracy. Dorothy Emmet shows how the quality of life operating through a civic culture – which includes education, religion, the arts, commerce and personal relationships – is the essential milieu for the practice of democracy. Where the quality of life is poor or non-existent, the democratic process will be weakened and may even be wiped out. British social democracy is thus very much about guaranteeing the conditions in which civilised political life can take place and democracy can develop. This accords with Roger Morgan's reminder to us that social democracy in its broadest sense is a movement that regards representative democracy as not merely instrumental (as socialists do) but as one of its essential values. Furthermore, the view emerged from a number of essays that our aim should not be 'Utopian'. As Dorothy Emmet puts it, 'it should not presuppose a society a long way removed from our own.' If this is accepted – as I think it should be by sensible reformers – it thus becomes possible to say that British social democrats are a *process* rather than a *panacea* party.

This, of course, may invite the charge of lack of idealism and I suspect there is some of that feeling abroad, particularly among the 'political virgins' who joined the party in the hope that it would lay a magic wand on all things and make them new. But we should not confuse idealism with ideology. The SDP has rejected from the outset any ideological model of the state. But it has pursued in a determined spirit the ideal of a more civilised, a more harmonious and a more prosperous society. Whatever vision we may have – and whatever priority we may attach to such things as wealth creation, wealth distribution, the arts, the countryside, defence and disarmament – there is an itchy feeling at the heart of social democracy that we are tantalisingly near the realisation of a wide range of beneficial objectives, of the sort that most people profess to want, yet whose achievement is blocked by great barriers of timidity, rigidity, factional blindness and unenlightened self-interest. And I would argue that an assault on the stronghold of all those vices, situated at Westminster and so staunchly defended by Labour and Conservative Parties alike, is no mean task and not without inspirational force.

Seen in this light Social Democracy becomes much more of a crusade than its commonsensical image suggests at first sight. This crusade demands effort and commitment and is frequently rewarded by rebuffs, setbacks and sometimes derision, but no one should doubt its strength because two things are on its side. There is an ineluctable trend in the direction of greater participation by the individual in decisions affecting his or her life; this is fuelled by the increase in leisure and the growth of political awareness. And there is a similar trend in the direction of greater accountability by official and quasi-official bodies under mounting public pressure. This is where the 'new politics' will be built. As regards objectives, Karl Popper said recently that the left has lost its programme because 'the former underdog has partly become the overdog or superdog, and partly even superman'. This creates a new situation in which there are new underdogs and new powers. The task of social democracy, he suggested, is to identify and assist these new underdogs and to fight these new powers – as all powers corrupt. That is in fact one of the fundamental aims of the SDP.

Social democracy, then, is very much about the reform of institutions, which it sees as a matter of urgency, and this includes economic institutions. Parliament is an economic institution of maximum importance in that budgets set the framework and devise the incentives within which a large part of economic activity takes place: if the citadel of parliament is occupied by a single party pursuing its own theory in the interests of its own financial backers, those incentives will be biased and that framework will be unjust. There are other institutions, notably corporations and unions, which largely decide and distort the apportionment of rewards through their arcane and elaborately confrontational bargaining procedures. Also, there is certainly a need for the reform of company law to recognise the role of contributors other than shareholders – and here I should like to pay tribute to the work done by George Goyder over the years in promoting the idea of the 'responsible company'. All this, I think, is pretty well common ground for social democrats and liberals. But there undoubtedly exists within our party an unease, voiced by Mark Goyder, that the SDP has stretched out too friendly a hand towards 'the market'. In his essay he used Ruskin as the vehicle of his critique and the subsequent discussion revealed the range of reactions to the phrase 'social market' current within the SDP, stretching from support to bewilderment and distaste. This phrase *is* ambiguous and I believe intentionally so: you can interpret it as importing market mechanisms into the delivery of social goods and services or, by insisting on the formulation 'social market economy', as Roger Morgan did, you can interpret it as advocating the pursuit of a successful market economy whose growth will allow for the provision of such services as most people in the country evidently agree should fall within the public domain.

Two things are at stake under either formulation: the extent of government intervention in the mainstream of the economy and the extent to which public services are sub-contracted to private suppliers. On the larger question, intervention of some sort follows naturally from the concern of social democrats about the huge accumulations of private market power, undreamed of by Smith, Bentham or Mill or indeed by anyone till Marx. All the 'middle way' solutions of the inter-war years were heavily tilted towards intervention and planning. The burden of David Marquand's critique was that all these solutions failed because it was airily assumed that they could be grafted on to existing political and economic structures without any change of the old order; the Webbs, Keynes and Evan Durbin all thought that a touch on the tiller by Oxbridge intellectuals could keep the grand plan on course. It never did. It is interesting, therefore, that the present tendency among reformers, whether liberals or social democrats, is away from heavy-handed intervention. This, however, does not mean that we have surrendered to *laissez-faire* but rather that our sights are set on the design or redesign of institutions in which market activity can properly and fairly take place without the exploitation of part-timers or the junking of whole workforces as a result of structural change in the economy with no chance of training or rehabilitation.

Similarly, on the question of the introduction of market mechanisms into public services, I think that social democrats will feel – certainly I feel – that it is absurd to order local authorities or health authorities to privatise their ancillary services; that is essentially a matter for local choice, which could properly be made within the context of proportional representation for local government. Thus, in the economic field as in the field of rights, we once again come back to institutional reform, involving here such things as bargaining procedures, arbitration, taxation, social security and so forth. You can debate the case for a minimum wage or a basic income guarantee, versus targeting help selectively, until the cows come home. But the key to 'economic justice' however defined is not enshrined in any of these formulae; it is to be located within a framework of just institutions, which command general support and within which competing claims can be argued out and compromises reached.

These are all, no doubt, enlightened and consoling thoughts but they are not of much avail as long as social democrats and liberals remain camped outside the citadel. I wrote earlier of an assault but that assault cannot, on reflection, be frontal; it cannot be an assault with ladders, surprising and overpowering the guard within the keep. The defences are too well manned by Conservative and Labour troops, wearing different uniforms but animated by one and the same thought: possession is ten points of the law. It therefore has to be done by a patient process of persuasion of the electorate that those inside, who have captured the constitution, should be obliged to return it to the people when they are finally obliged to lower the drawbridge at the end of their tenure; the five-year maximum lease is the one constitutional convention that does still *just* hold. And perhaps the best way of persuading the British public is by demonstrating that *neither* of the main candidates for the keys of the citadel of democracy is ultimately democratic.

Danny Finkelstein demonstrated this in relation to the Labour Party. Taking the 'incoherence' remarked on by David Marquand and the 'malign ambiguity' revealed by Robert Skidelsky a stage further, he showed that 'to believe in a perfect society is to believe in "conservatism deferred" – the possibility of building a society that no one will want to change'. Such a belief carries in its heart the implication that once the goal is achieved, liberal democracy can be quietly dumped. That is the belief of the hard left. Revisionists are, on the best interpretation, simply confused. It is in this essay, also, that the unique role of the working class as the agent of change is exposed as the doctrinaire and sentimental piece of unreality it is. And here the word 'classless' – which also, to be fair, smacks of unreality – in the SDP's constitution suddenly acquires meaning: it does not mean stifling uniformity or absolute equality of outcome; it indicates rather that progress in politics through 'the class war' is dead.

Turning to the Conservatives, I revert to the introduction, in which I accepted that the New Right had occupied the commanding heights of the political agenda for more than a decade. I now think 'commanding heights' is too grand an expression for the entrenchment of self-interest in government. And here again the commitment to democracy is far from convincing. As Nick Bosanquet's essay

shows, there is a strong belief among the New Right that the
political system is a far less successful method of making choices
than 'the market' and would, in an ideal world, be eliminated; 'The
right to vote is largely an unfortunate historical accident; in any
sane community it will become increasingly redundant as people
gain their goals through market processes. In practice, political
authority may become a despotism tempered by middle-class pressure groups.' Thus, in the New Right's exaltation of 'the market' as
the *sole* mechanism for family and individual expression and choice,
we have the mirror image of Labour's Utopia, in which democratic
politics will also wither away.

Against this disturbing prospect, implicit both in Conservative
and in Labour philosophy, social democracy advances the following
antithesis: that political rights and their exercise are the main means
of redressing the imbalance between consumers and producers in a
world of increasingly powerful producer groups; that private coercion can be as much of a threat as public coercion and a framework
is needed and always will be needed to contain the excesses of both
private and public power; that the entrepreneur has indeed a crucial
role to play in society – this was Schumpeter's message – but is
dependent on the contributions of many people at many points in
the production process who cannot be marginalised; that capitalism
in the long run does increase aggregate wealth, but the effect of
rapid and unforeseen economic change cannot be insured against by
its ordinary victims, whose involuntary sacrifices must be compen-
sated. On equality, social democracy accepts that some inequalities
are inevitable and even 'serviceable' in John Rawls's phrase, but
those that are not serviceable have no place in a civilised society. On
poverty, social democrats condemn the refusal of the New Right to
recognise anything but absolute poverty (even Adam Smith
accepted that 'necessaries' were relative); the relief of poverty on the
minimalist notion of preventing starvation will only lead to the ever
greater dependency of a growing 'underclass' of unemployables on
the state – the very opposite of what Conservatives profess to want.
On remedies, social democracy will pull out all the stops: there is no
room for a public monopoly of the welfare state.

When these brave words have been uttered, it is incumbent on all
those associated with the enterprise of British social democracy to
accept that it will be a long haul yet. We are after all, as I have said,
a party of process and not of panaceas. Some of the concerns

expressed in this book may seem abstruse and frankly recondite to the average apolitical person, who has not unnaturally accepted conventional wisdom on British freedoms and the supremacy of the Mother of Parliaments. But the less conventional wisdom embodied in these essays is founded, in my belief and that of my associates, on an analysis of British ills that must by its inner logic lead sooner or later to the surrender of the usurped citadel by the unjust Prince.

Roger Morgan pp. 1–18

An earlier version of this chapter appeared in *Government and Opposition*, Vol. 17, No. 1 (Winter 1982). Extracts from that version are reproduced here by kind permission of the editors.

1 Bertrand Russell, *German Social Democracy*, London, 1896, new edition 1965, p. 1.
2 Anthony Crosland, *Social Democracy in Europe*, Fabian Tract 438, London, 1975.
3 David Marquand, *Russet-Coated Captains: the Challenge of Social Democracy*, Open Forum Series No. 5, London, 1981, p. 4.
4 Crosland, *op. cit.*, especially pp. 1, 10, 12.
5 Karl Marx, *Critique of the Gotha Programme* (1875). For background see Roger Morgan, *The German Social Democrats and the First International*, Cambridge, 1965, and the classic study by Arthur Rosenberg, *Democracy and Socialism: A Contribution to the Political History of the Last 150 Years*, London, 1939.
6 See James Joll, *The Second International*, London, 1955.
7 Bertrand Russell, *German Social Democracy*, London, 1896, new edition 1965.
8 Crosland, *op. cit.*, p. 3, stresses the social democratic commitment to pursue social justice and equality by means of a mixed economy and 'liberty, democracy and the rule of law'.
9 A penetrating analysis of this problem is given by Douglas Webber in *The Future of Social Democracy*, ed. William E. Paterson and Alastair H. Thomas, Oxford, 1986.

David Marquand pp. 19–33

1 For the neo-liberal explanation, see in particular Sam Brittan, *The Economic Consequences of Democracy*, London, 1977 and *The Role and Limits of Government: Essays in Political Economy*, London, 1983. For the neo-socialist version, see Ian Gough, *The Political Economy of the Welfare State*, London, 1979.
2 Politics have, of course, been as polarised in France as in Britain for much of the post-war period; but since the socialist victory in 1981, they seem to have become less polarised than a decade earlier, whereas in Britain the trend has been in the other direction.
3 An important exception is Peter Clarke, *Liberals and Social Democrats*, Cambridge, 1978.
4 For this transformation see David Landes, *The Unbound Prometheus*, Cambridge, 1969.
5 L.T. Hobhouse, *Liberalism*, London, 1911, p. 123.
6 *Ibid.*, pp. 163–4.

7 Liberal Party, *Britain's Industrial Future: being the Report of the Liberal Industrial Inquiry of 1928*, London, second impression 1977.

8 Robert Boothby *et al*, *Industry and the State: A Conservative View*, London, 1927.

9 Harold Macmillan, *The Middle Way: A Study of the Economic and Social Progress in a Free and Democratic Society*, London, 1966 edition, p. 190.

10 *Ibid.*, chapters X to XIII.

11 Evan Durbin, *The Politics of Democratic Socialism: An Essay on Social Policy*, London, 1957 impression.

12 Elizabeth Durbin, *New Jerusalems, The Labour Party and the Economics of Democratic Socialism*, London, 1985.

13 Anthony Crosland, *The Future of Socialism*, London, 1956, p. 112.

14 *Ibid.*, p. 380.

15 Leo Pliatzky, *Getting and Spending: Public Expenditure, Employment and Inflation*, Oxford, paperback edition 1984, p. 146.

16 Keith Middlemass, *Politics in Industrial Society: The Experience of the British System since 1911*, André Deutsch, London, 1979, pp. 152–244.

George Goyder pp. 34–43

1 *The Wealth of Nations (WN)*, ed. Cannan, 1904, Bk. V, p. 259.

2 The Theory of Moral Sentiments (*TMS*), Oxford, 1976, p. 85.

3 *TMS*, p. 86.

4 Montesquieu, *L'Esprit des Lois*, Bk. III, ch. iii.

5 *TMS*, pp. 184–5.

6 *WN*, Bk. IV, p. 168.

7 Arthur Bryant, *English Saga (1840–1940)*, London, 1940, p. 215.

8 *WN*, Bk. IV, p. 421.

9 *WN*, Bk. V, p. 377.

10 Jacob Viner, *Adam Smith 1776–1926*, Chicago, 1928, p. 149.

11 *WN*, Bk. II, p. 338.

12 J.M. Keynes, *The General Theory of Employment, Interest and Money*, London, 1973, p. 351.

13 R.H. Tawney, *A Discourse upon Usury*, London, 1925.

14 *WN*, Bk. I, p. 249.

15 *WN*, Bk. IV, p. 419.

16 *WN*, Bk. IV, p. 175.

17 *WN*, Bk. IV, p. 159.

18 *WN*, Bk. IV, pp. 457–8.

19 *WN*. Bk I, p. 1.

20 *WN*, Bk. I, p. 12.

21 *WN*, Bk. V, p. 266.

22 *WN*, Bk. V, p. 267.

23 *WN*, Bk. V, p. 267.

24 Sir Henry Phelps Brown, in *The Market and the State: Essays in Honour of Adam Smith*, eds T. Wilson and A. Skinner, Oxford, 1976, p. 251.

25 *WN*, Bk. I, p. 83.

Alan Ryan pp. 44–57

1 Alan Ryan, *The Philosophy of John Stuart Mill*, London, 1970, 2nd ed. 1987; John Gray, *Mill On Liberty: A Defence*, London, 1983.
2 'The Probable Futurity of the Labouring Classes', *Principles of Political Economy*, IV, vii, *Collected Works of John Stuart Mill*, Toronto, 1963– vol. III, pp. 758–96.
3 Elie Halévy, *The Growth of Philosophical Radicalism*, London, 1928, p. 249; but see William Thomas, *The Philosophic Radicals*, Oxford, 1979 for a subtler, more sceptical view.
4 'Bentham', *Collected Works*, vol. X, pp. 77–115.
5 Gertrude Himmelfarb, 'The Haunted House of Jeremy Bentham', *Victorian Minds*, London, 1968, pp. 32–81.
6 See e.g. the discussion of punishment in *An Introduction to the Principles of Morals and Legislation*, London, 1970, pp. 156ff.
7 Mill, *Collected Works*, X, p. 113.
8 'Considerations on Representative Government', *Collected Works*, XIX, pp. 403–12.
9 'On Liberty', *Collected Works*, XVIII, p. 224.
10 *Collected Works*, XVIII, p. 223.
11 'The Subjection of Women', *Collected Works*, XX, pp. 336–7.
12 'Representative Government', *Collected Works*, XIX, pp. 488–9.
13 On inheritance, see *Principles*, II, ii, 3, *Collected Works*, vol. II, pp. 218–26.

Mark Goyder pp. 58–71

1 William Morris, 'How I became a Socialist', in *William Morris' Collected Writings*, ed. Asa Briggs, Harmondsworth, 1962.
2 *Unto This Last* (*UTL*), Kings Treasuries edition, London, p. 20.
3 *UTL*, p. 23.
4 *UTL*, p. 29.
5 *UTL*, p. 45.
6 *UTL*, p. 45.
7 *UTL*, p. 56.
8 *UTL*, p. 57.
9 *UTL*, p. 81.
10 *UTL*, p. 92.
11 *UTL*, p. 93.
12 *UTL*, p. 97.
13 *UTL*, p. 102.
14 *UTL*, p. 101.
15 *UTL*, p. 113.
16 *UTL*, p. 116.
17 J.A. Hobson, *John Ruskin, Social Reformer*, 1898, p. 65.
18 Martin Wiener, *English Culture and the Decline of the Industrial Spirit*, Harmondsworth, 1985, p. 39.
19 *UTL*, p. 37.
20 Quoted in *Management Today*, January 1986, p. 61.
21 J.A. Hobson, *op. cit.*, p. 143.

Robert Skidelsky pp. 72–97

1 'Liberalism and Labour', *Nation*, 9 February 1926; in *The Collected Writings of John Maynard Keynes (CW)*, ix, 309. All references to Keynes's printed works will be to the *CW* edition, preceded by place and date of original appearance.

2 'Democracy and Efficiency', *New Statesman*, 28 January 1939; *CW*, xxi, 500.

3 'The End of Laissez-Faire', Sidney Ball Lecture, Oxford, November 1924; *CW*, ix, 292.

4 Notably in 'The Dilemma of Modern Socialism', *Political Quarterly*, April–June 1932; *CW*, xxi, 33–48.

5 Elizabeth Durbin, *New Jerusalems*, 1985, p. 11.

6 Bertrand Russell, *Autobiography*, i, 1967, p. 71.

7 JMK, 'The Political Doctrines of Edmund Burke', 1904; in Keynes Papers, Marshall Library.

8 *Ibid.*, pp. 16–17, 95.

9 *Ibid.*, pp. 28–9.

10 *Ibid.*, p. 49.

11 *Economic Consequences; CW*, ii, 6.

12 *A Tract on Monetary Reform*, 1923, *CW*, iv, 56–7.

13 *Burke*, pp. 60–9.

14 *Ibid.*, pp. 11–12.

15 *Ibid.*, p. 14.

16 See for example, Tony Lawson and Hashem Pesaran, eds, *Keynes' Economics: Methodological Issues*, 1985.

17 *General Theory; CW*, vii, 381.

18 *Essays in Persuasion*, Preface; *CW*, ix, xviii.

19 John Strachey, *The Coming Struggle for Power*, 1933, 200ff.

20 *General Theory*; *CW*, vii, 384.

21 'Reconstruction in Europe: An Introduction', *Manchester Guardian Commercial*, 18 May 1922; *CW*, xvii, 427.

22 Seymour Harris, *John Maynard Keynes*, 1955, p. 79.

23 *General Theory; CW*, vii, p. 378.

24 *E.g.*, JMK to E.F.M. Durbin, 30 April 1936; *CW*, xxix, 235. However, the idea of monetary fine-tuning comes mainly from before the *General Theory*.

25 *General Theory; CW*, vii, 164.

26 *CW*, xix, 347.

27 'Mr. Keynes Replies to Shaw', *New Statesman*, 10 November 1934; *CW*, xxviii, 32.

28 Letter to the *Westminster Gazette*, 17 July 1926; *CW*, xix, 567–8.

29 *CW*, xx, 263.

30 Address to the Liberal Summer School, *Manchester Guardian*, 1 August 1927; *CW*, xix, 696.

31 'The End of Laissez-Faire'; *CW*, ix, 289.

32 C.A.R. Crosland, *The Future of Socialism*, 1964 edition, 15ff.

33 *CW*, xix, 697.

34 'Am I a Liberal?', *CW*, ix, 295–6.
35 *Ibid.*, p. 299.
36 'The End of Laissez-Faire'; *CW*, ix, 290.
37 'Am I a Liberal?'; *CW*, ix, 297.
38 Elizabeth Johnson, 'John Maynard Keynes: Scientist or Politician?', in Joan Robinson, ed., *After Keynes*, 1973, p. 24.
39 *CW*, ix, 289.
40 JMK to G.B. Shaw, 1 January 1935; *CW*, xiii, 492.
41 'A Short View of Soviet Russia', Hogarth Press, December 1925; *CW*, ix, 253–71.
42 'Democracy and Efficiency'; *CW*, xxi, 494–5.
43 See esp. 'The Dilemma of Modern Socialism'; *CW*, xxi, 33–48.
44 'The End of Laissez-Faire'; *CW*, ix, 291–2.
45 *General Theory*; *CW*, vii, 378–9.
46 Speech to League of Nations Union Conference on Unemployment, March 1924; *CW*, xix, 184.
47 *General Theory; CW*, vii, 370.

Inigo Bing and Kevin Carey pp. 98–112

1 John Rawls, *A Theory of Justice*, Oxford, 1972.
2 Ronald Dworkin, *Taking Rights Seriously*, London, 1977.
3 Ronald Dworkin, *A Matter of Principle*, Massachusetts, 1985.
4 These two principles are a special conception of a general conception which is: 'All social values – liberty and opportunity, income and wealth, and the bases of self respect – are to be distributed equally unless an unequal distribution of any, or all, of these values is to be to everyone's advantage.' However the general conception only applies in the early stages of social and economic development and is therefore not strictly relevant to this essay.
5 *A Theory of Justice*, p. 11.
6 *Ibid.*, p. 511.
7 *Taking Rights Seriously*, p. 182.
8 Henry Sidgwick, *Methods of Ethics*, London, 1907.
9 *A Theory of Justice*, pp.183–92 and Section 30: 'Classical Utilitarianism'.
10 Ronald Dworkin has commented: 'The liberal needs a scheme of civil rights whose effect will be to determine those political decisions that are antecedently likely to reflect strong external preferences and to remove those decisions from majoritarian political institutions altogether.' This argument is fully developed in Part III of *A Matter of Principle op. cit.*, entitled 'Liberalism and Justice', and Chapter 9, 'Reverse Discrimination', in *Taking Rights Seriously op. cit.*
11 *A Matter of Principle*, p. 198, and the argument in Chapter 8, 'Liberalism'.

Dorothy Emmet pp. 113–28

1 D. Emmet, *The Moral Roots of Social Democracy*, Tawney Publication

No. 26. This pamphlet contains a fuller treatment of the topic of the present paper. I am grateful to the Tawney Society and its secretary Tony Flower for permission to draw on it.

2 *Philosophy and Public Affairs*, Summer 1985, p. 237.
3 R. Dahrendorf, *A Divided Society*, Tawney Publication No. 29.
4 R. Scruton, *The Meaning of Conservatism*, Harmondsworth, 1980, p. 6.
5 *Ibid.*, p. 53.

Danny Finkelstein pp. 129–35

1 David Owen, *Face the Future*, London, 1981.
2 Institute of Economic Affairs, *Agenda for Social Democracy*, London, 1983.
3 Ed. M.I. Cole, *Beatrice Webb Diaries 1912–24*, London, 1952.
4 David Owen, *Ownership: The Way Forward*, Open Forum Pamphlet, 1985.
5 Elizabeth Durbin, *New Jerusalems: The Labour Party and the Economics of Democratic Socialism*, London, 1985.
6 David Marquand, *Ramsay MacDonald*, London, 1981.
7 Philip Williams, *Hugh Gaitskell*, Oxford, 1982.
8 John Vaizey, *In Breach of Promise*, London, 1983.
9 For example, Karl Popper, *The Open Society and its Enemies*, London, 1945. (Bryan Magee's brilliant book *Popper*, London, 1973, should be compulsory reading for social democrats.)
10 Anthony Crosland, *The Future of Socialism*, London, 1956.
11 Adolf Berle and Gardiner Means, *The Modern Corporation and Private Property*, 1933.
12 Evan Durbin, *The Politics of Democratic Socialism*, Labour Book Service, 1940.

Nick Bosanquet pp. 136–51

1 Nick Bosanquet, *After the New Right*, Heinemann, London, 1983, sets these out more fully.
2 A. Smith, *The Theory of Moral Sentiments*, Oxford, 1976, p. 269.
3 David Hume, 'Of the Origin of Government' in H.D. Aiken (ed.) *Hume's Moral and Political Philosophy*, New York, 1972, pp. 97–101.
4 Lord Robbins, *Liberty and Equality*, IEA Occasional Paper, No. 52, 1977.

NOTES ON CONTRIBUTORS

Inigo Bing is a barrister who read law at Birmingham university. He is a member of the Committee of the Tawney Society. *Kevin Carey* read history at Cambridge and was a Knox Scholar at Harvard studying under John Rawls. Their pamphlet 'Unveiling the Right, the philosophy of John Rawls' was published by the Tawney Society in 1985.

Nick Bosanquet is an economist with interests in social economics. He is currently Senior Research Fellow at the Centre for Health Economics, University of York. Author of *After the New Right*, he has also published studies of NHS funding and of how family doctors take decisions.

Dorothy Emmet was Professor of Philosophy in the University of Manchester. She is now retired in Cambridge. Her books include *Function, Purpose and Powers; Rules, Roles and Relations; The Moral Prism* and *The Effectiveness of Causes*.

Daniel Finkelstein was educated at the LSE and City University Business School and is currently researching high technology policy. He was National Chair of the Young Social Democrats (1983–5) and is a member of the SDP National and Policy Committees.

George Goyder CBE was managing director of British International Paper Ltd (1935–72) and Controller of Newsprint during the war. Joint founder of the British-North American Committee, he is author of *The Responsible Company* (1961) and *The Responsible Worker* (1975).

Mark Goyder is a distribution manager in the paper industry. Deputy leader of the Alliance Group on Kent County Council, he is also an occasional columnist for *The Times* and a founder of the Tawney Society for which he has written pamphlets on industrial partnership and a national community volunteer scheme.

Alastair Kilmarnock is deputy leader of the SDP peers and their spokesman on health, social services and social security; he is a member of the SDP National and Policy Committees. As Alastair Boyd he is the author of a number of travel books.

David Marquand was a Labour MP for eleven years, then a chief adviser in the European Commission, before taking up his present post as Professor of Politics at Salford University. He has been a member of the SDP National Committee since 1981. His books include *Ramsay MacDonald* and *Parliament for Europe*.

Roger Morgan, now a Research Fellow at the Centre for International Studies at the LSE, has been deputy director of studies at the Royal Institute of International Affairs, Head of the European Centre for Political Studies and lecturer or professor at several British and American universities. His books include *Western Europe since 1945: the Shaping of the European Community* (1973) and *Partners and Rivals in Western Europe: Britain, France, and Germany* (co-edited with Caroline Bray, 1986).

Alan Ryan has been fellow and tutor in Politics at New College, Oxford, since 1969; FBA 1986. He is the author of *The Philosophy of John Stuart Mill* (2nd edition 1987) and *Property and Political Theory* (1984). His *Bertrand Russell's Radicalism* will appear later this year.

Robert Skidelsky is Professor of International Studies, University of Warwick, and author of *Politicians and the Slump* (1967); *English Progressive Schools* (1970); *Oswald Mosley* (1975) and *John Maynard Keynes*, vol. I (1983); he is also a founder member of the SDP.